by Sandy Feldstein and Larry Clark

Musicianship from Day One

Welcome to the Yamaha Advantage™ Book 2

Congratulations on completing Book 1. This book will continue your music education in a way that will be fun. The Yamaha Advantage contains music of all cultures and all styles from rock to classical, to provide you with a wide variety of enjoyable music to play. Everything you need to know to play your instrument is included and reinforced so you will continue to become a proficient musician. If you have a computer, you can visit www.yamahaadvantage.com, a Web site designed to help you learn more and have more fun.

The recorded accompaniments available separately or downloadable from the Web site are recorded by a great band. They will provide hours of enjoyable play-along experiences and let you hear professional musicians playing the music contained in your book.

Whether your goal is to be in a rock band, a symphony orchestra or just to learn to play an instrument, we know the Yamaha Advantage will help you get there.

Have a great time making music.

Sandy Feldstein   Larry Clark

About Your Book

The Yamaha Advantage™ is designed to look like a computer screen — like an Internet Web site. The "buttons" at the top of each page show the concepts you will learn throughout the method. Everything new at the top of the page is presented with a colorful drop-down menu. Each exercise that reinforces those concepts is highlighted with a corresponding color. For example, if a new note is introduced, it is shown in a red drop-down menu. The number of the exercise that first uses that note is also highlighted in red.

Throughout the Yamaha Advantage you will see a picture of a hand pointing to extra exercises which appear at the back of the book. Use these exercises for additional practice.

CARL FISCHER®
65 Bleecker Street, New York, NY 10012

Graphic System Development,
Design and Illustration: Susan Blakely
Additional Art and Layout Design for
Book 2: Jorge Paredes
Engraver: Mark Ralston

YBM202

ISBN 0-8258-4616-1

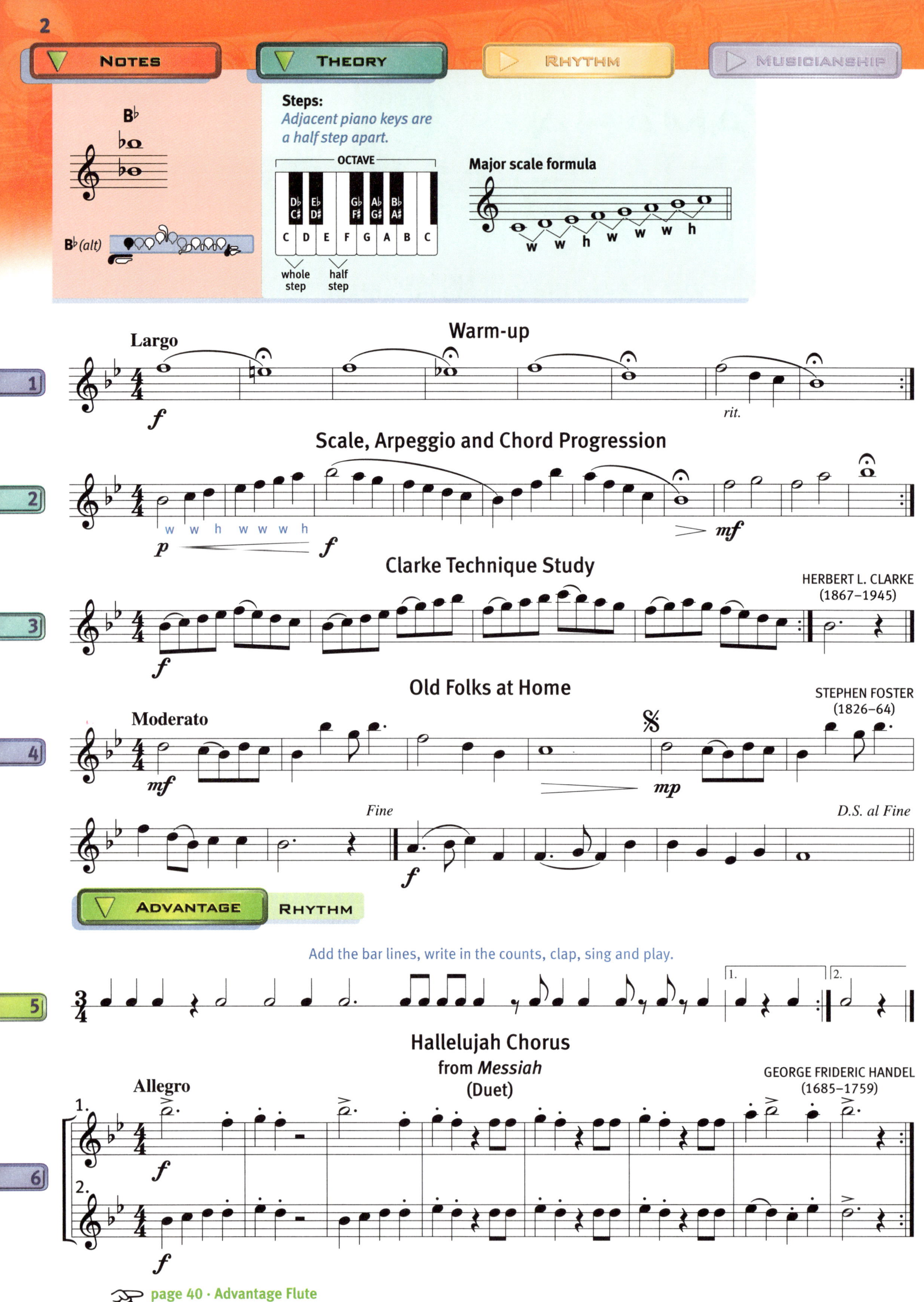
2
NOTES
THEORY
RHYTHM
MUSICIANSHIP
B♭
B♭ (alt)
Steps:
Adjacent piano keys are a half step apart.
OCTAVE
D♭ C♯
E♭ D♯
G♭ F♯
A♭ G♯
B♭ A♯
C D E F G A B C
whole step
half step
Major scale formula
w w h w w w h
Warm-up
Largo
1
f
rit.
Scale, Arpeggio and Chord Progression
2
w w h w w w h
p
f
mf
Clarke Technique Study
HERBERT L. CLARKE (1867–1945)
3
f
Old Folks at Home
STEPHEN FOSTER (1826–64)
Moderato
4
mf
mp
Fine
D.S. al Fine
f
ADVANTAGE
RHYTHM
Add the bar lines, write in the counts, clap, sing and play.
5
1.
2.
Hallelujah Chorus
from Messiah
(Duet)
GEORGE FRIDERIC HANDEL (1685–1759)
Allegro
6
1.
2.
f
f
page 40 · Advantage Flute
YBM202

Notes
Theory
Rhythm
Musicianship
A major chord contains the 1st, 3rd and 5th notes of a major scale.
C scale
C chord
1 2 3 4 5 6 7 8
In the Bleak Midwinter
(Chorale)
GUSTAV HOLST
(1874–1934)
Andante
p
rit.
Scale, Arpeggio and Chord Progression
Chord
p
f
1 3 5
mf
Klosé Technique Study
HYACINTHE-ELÉONORE KLOSÉ
(1808–80)
f
Cockles and Mussels
Moderato
Irish Folk Song
mf legato
f
p
f
Advantage
Play by Ear · Alouette
French-Canadian Folk Song
f
Now try playing this song starting on F.
Kaeru No Uta
Frog Song
(Round)
A.
Allegro
B.
Japanese Folk Song
mp
C.
D.

page 38 · Advantage Rhythm

Chester
(Chorale)

0 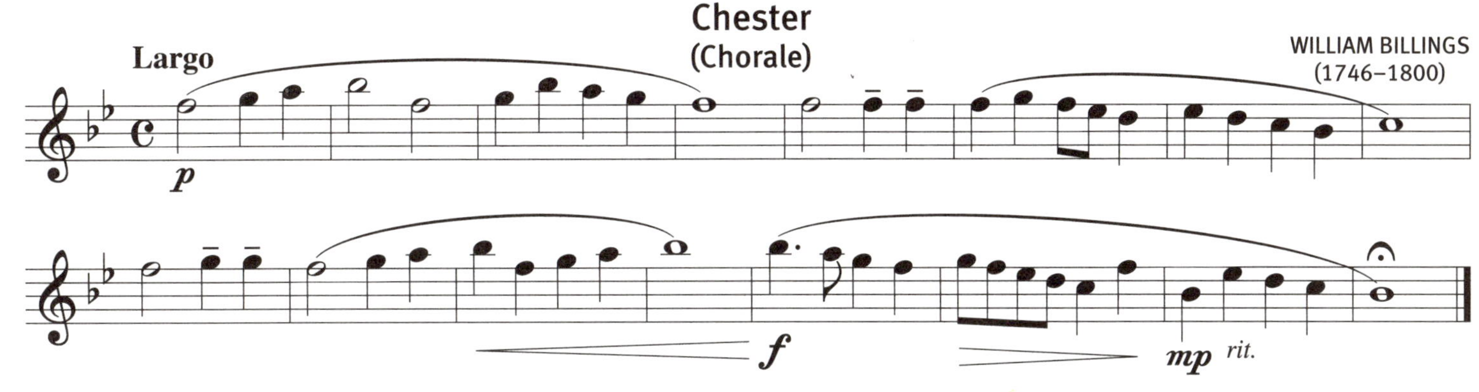

Dance of the Tumblers
from *Snow Maiden*

1 

Czech Dance

2 

Chords are built on the first, fourth and fifth notes of the major scale.

Using the notes of the chords, compose or improvise a melody using any rhythms you know. Add phrase markings, tempo and dynamics, then play your composition.

3 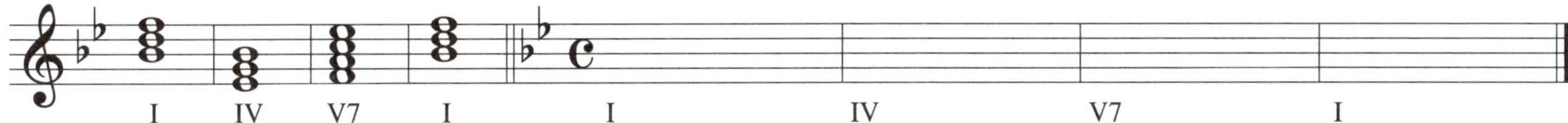

Smooth Move
(Duet)

4 

page 38 · Advantage Rhythm

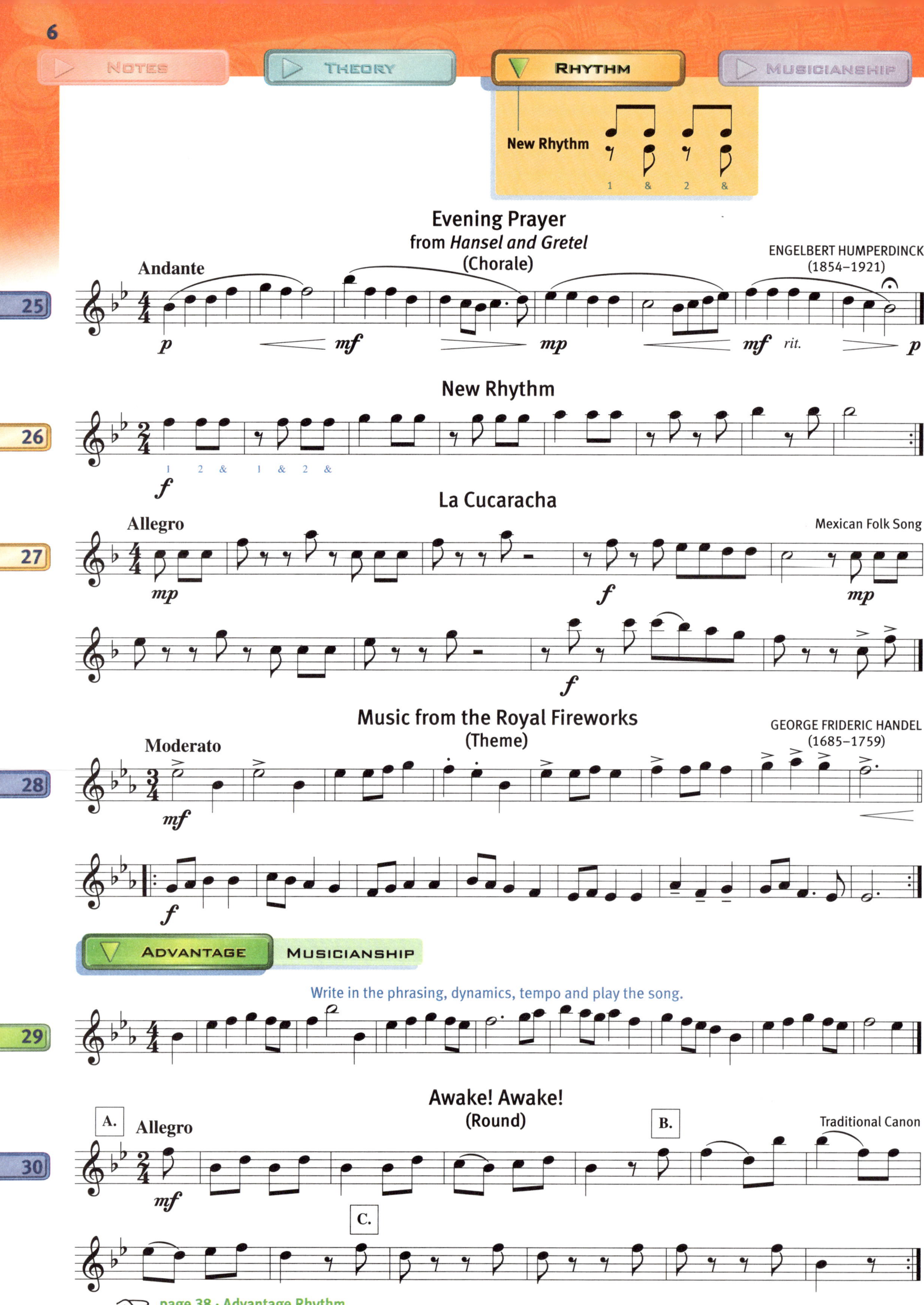

page 38 · Advantage Rhythm

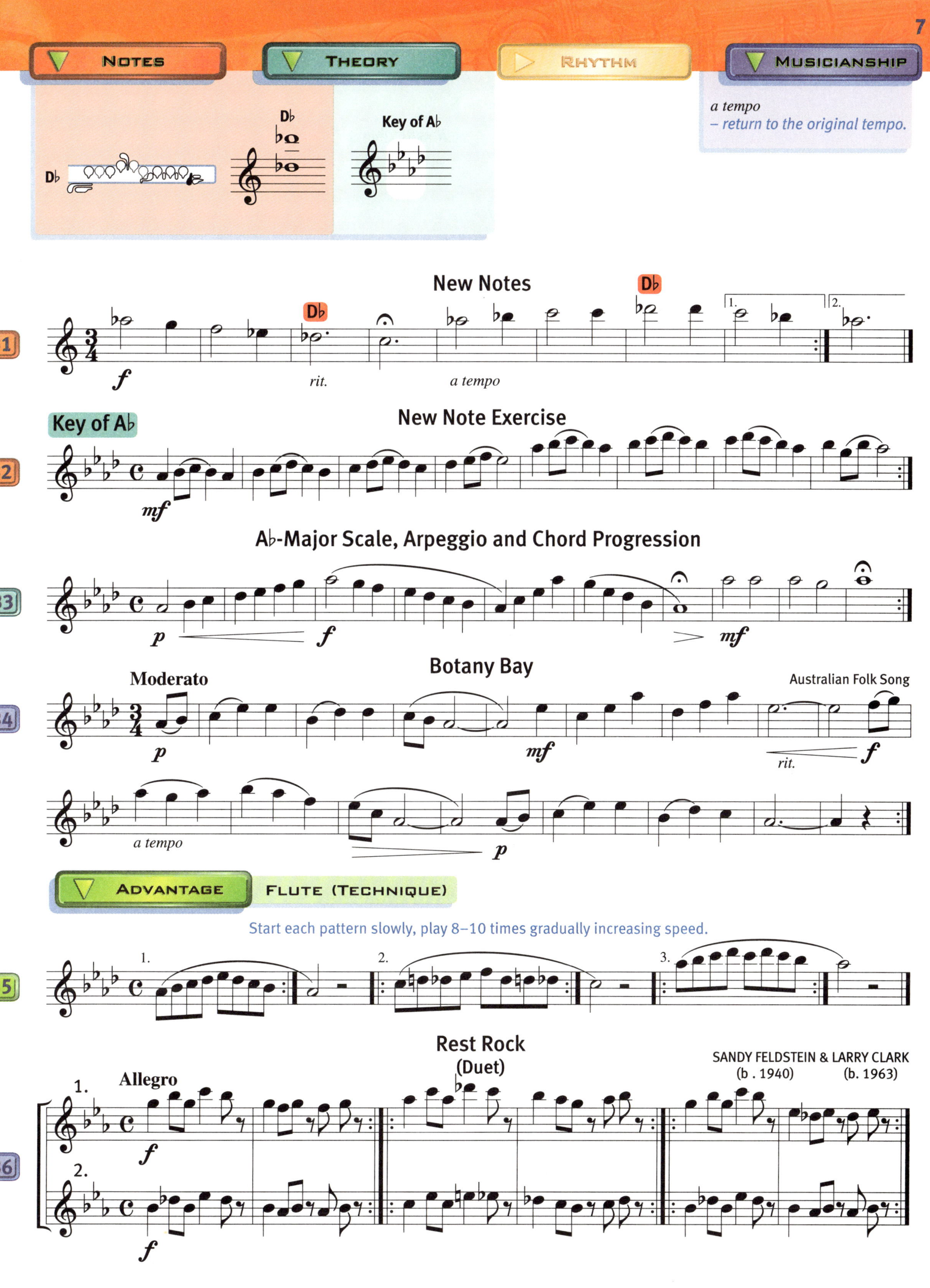
NOTES
THEORY
RHYTHM
MUSICIANSHIP
D♭
D♭
Key of A♭
a tempo
– return to the original tempo.
New Notes
31
D♭
D♭
f
rit.
a tempo
1.
2.
Key of A♭
New Note Exercise
32
mf
A♭-Major Scale, Arpeggio and Chord Progression
33
p
f
mf
Botany Bay
34
Moderato
Australian Folk Song
p
mf
rit.
f
a tempo
p
ADVANTAGE
FLUTE (TECHNIQUE)
Start each pattern slowly, play 8–10 times gradually increasing speed.
35
1.
2.
3.
Rest Rock
(Duet)
SANDY FELDSTEIN & LARRY CLARK
(b . 1940)
(b. 1963)
36
Allegro
1.
2.
f
f

New Rhythm
Syncopation
1 & 2 &

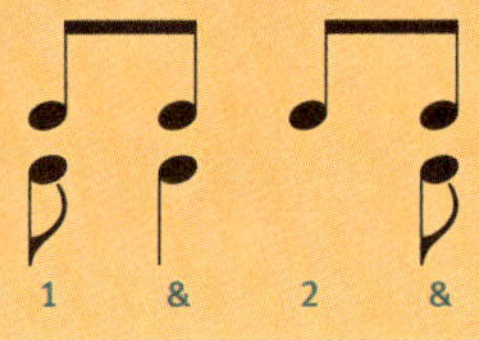

Doxology
(Chorale)

LOUIS BOURGEOIS
(ca. 1510–61)

37 Largo *mf* *f* *rit.*

New Rhythm

38 1 & 2 & 1 & 2 & *mf*

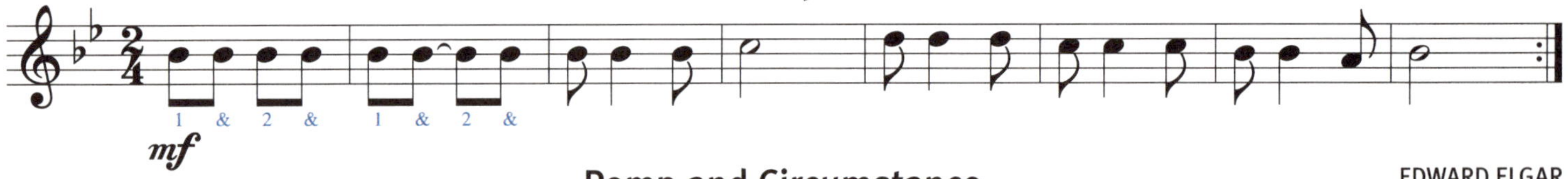

Pomp and Circumstance

EDWARD ELGAR
(1857–1934)

39 Andante *mp* *legato* *mf* 1. 2. *f*

ADVANTAGE THEORY (SCALE & CHORDS)

Write the F scale, indicate the whole and half steps, write the note names, then fill in the missing notes of the F chord.

40 F W F chord

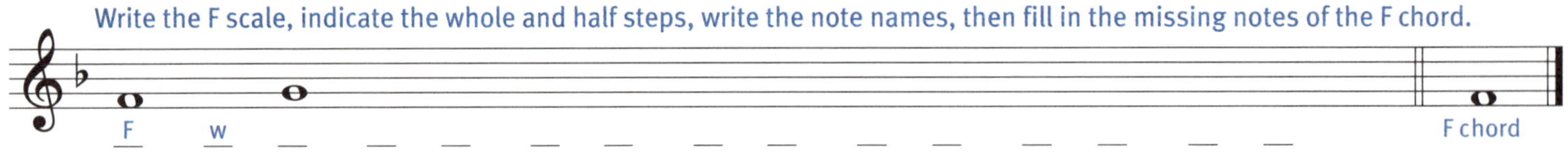

Give My Regards to Broadway
(Mini-Piece)

GEORGE M. COHAN
(1878–1942)

41 Moderato *f*

11

19

27 *div.*

page 38 · Advantage Rhythm

Colonel Bogey

KENNETH J. ALFORD
(1881–1945)
arranged by Sandy Feldstein & Larry Clark

Moderate March Tempo

unis. *f* 5 *p-f* 21 1. 2.

Latin Serenade

SANDY FELDSTEIN & LARRY CLARK
(b.1940) (b.1963)

Moderato 4 5 second time only *mf* 1. 2. *f* *Fine* *div.* *mp* 16 1. 2. 26 *unis.* *f* 34 4 *D.S. al Fine*

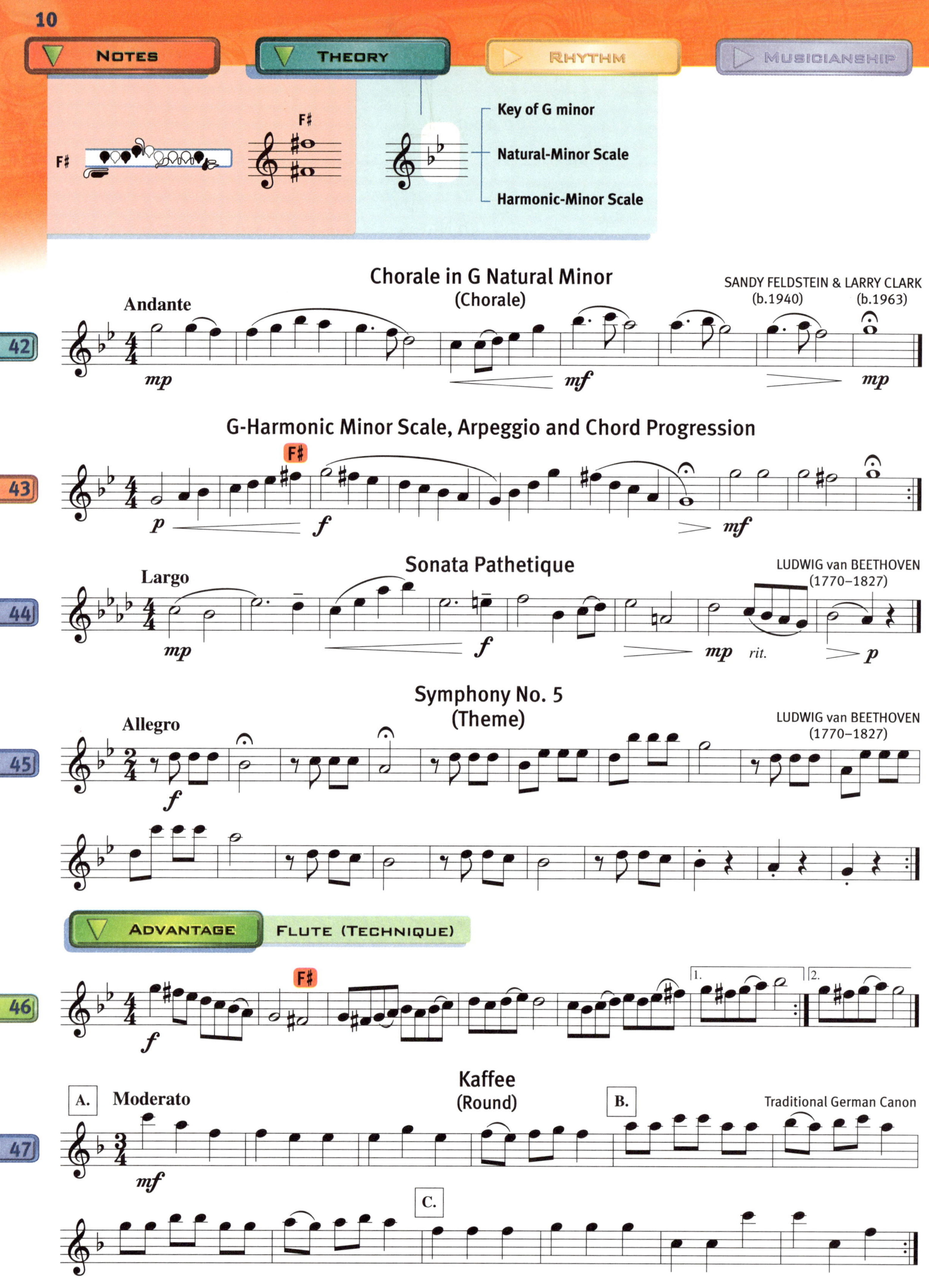

page 38 · Advantage Rhythm

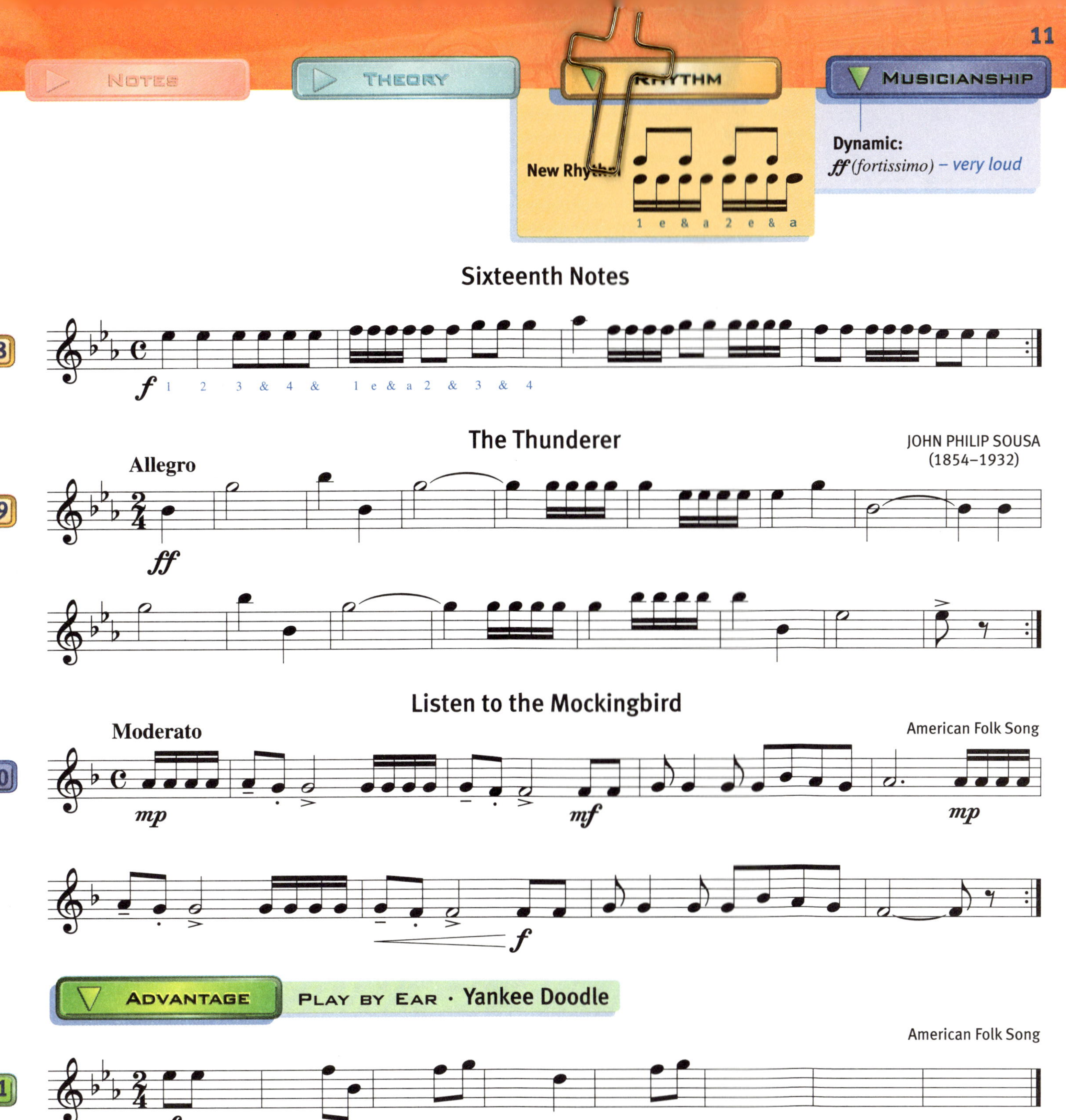

Now try playing this song starting on F.

Call and Response
(Mini-Piece)

African Folk Song

Allegro

2

Solo/Soli *p* · Tutti *mp* · Solo/Soli · Tutti div. *mf* · Solo/Soli unis. · Tutti div. *f*

Solo/Soli unis. · Tutti div. *ff* · Solo/Soli unis. *p* · Tutti *f* · div. *ff*

page 38 · Advantage Rhythm

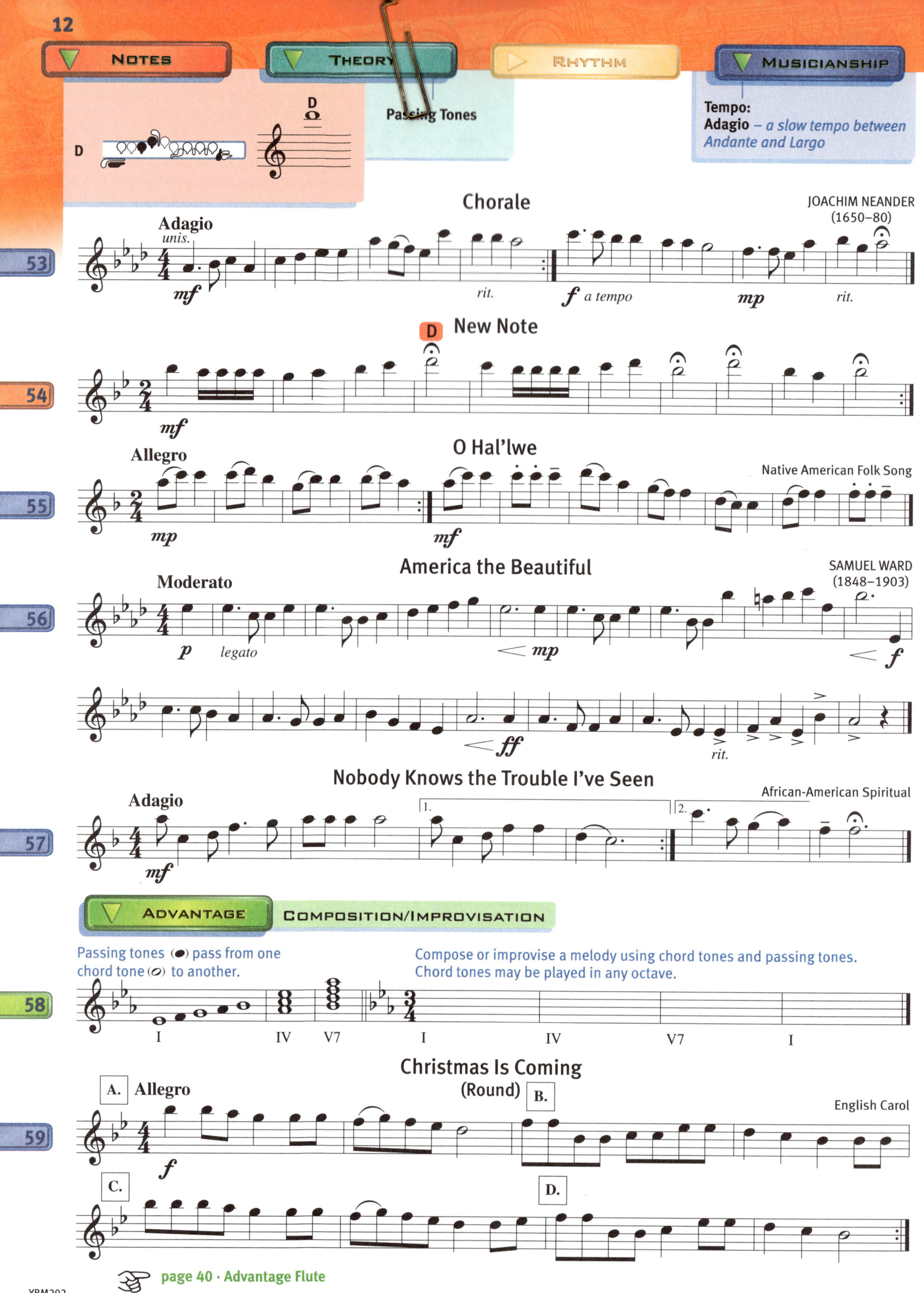

page 40 · Advantage Flute

page 38 · Advantage Rhythm

NOTES
THEORY
RHYTHM
MUSICIANSHIP
B
D♭
Key of C minor
Tempo:
Allegretto – moderately fast
Chorale in C Natural Minor
Largo
66
mp
mf
mp
mf
p
C-Harmonic Minor Scale, Arpeggio and Chord Progression
67
p
f
mf
Scarborough Fair
English Folk Song
Allegretto
68
p
legato
mf
f
mf
p
Liza Jane
African-American Folk Song
Allegro
69
f
1.
2.
ADVANTAGE
TRUMPET (EMBOUCHURE EXERCISE)
70
Thou, Poor Bird
(Round)
A.
Moderato
B.
C.
D.
English Folk Song
71
mp

New Rhythm

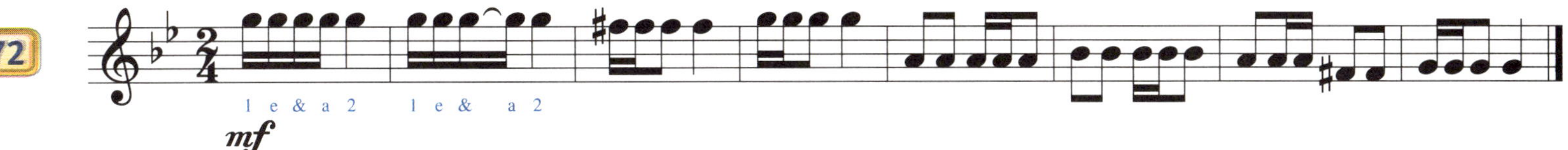

Dinah

American Folk Song

Valse

JOHANNES BRAHMS
(1833–97)

ADVANTAGE RHYTHM

Write in the counts, clap, sing and play.

Eine Kleine Nachtmusik
(Mini-Piece)

WOLFGANG AMADEUS MOZART
(1756–91)

page 38 · Advantage Rhythm, page 40 · Advantage Flute

Adeste Fideles
JOHN F. WADE
(1711–86)
arranged by Sandy Feldstein & Larry Clark
Andante
mf
5
mp
legato
13
f
rit.
Fine
a tempo
mf
25
mf
33
div.
f
unis.
D.S. al Fine
Can-Can
from Orpheus in the Underworld
JACQUES OFFENBACH
(1819–80)
arranged by Sandy Feldstein & Larry Clark
Allegro
mp
f
5
mp
13
3
f
mf
3
21
mp
p
27
mf
ff
34
mf
ff

NOTES · THEORY · RHYTHM · MUSICIANSHIP

B
C
D

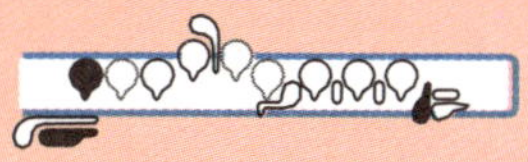

Key of C

Key of C Major

Chorale in C

SANDY FELDSTEIN & LARRY CLARK
(b.1940) (b.1963)

77 Adagio *div.* *mp* *unis.* B *rit.* *div.* *mf a tempo* *f* *unis.* *rit.* *mp*

Scale, Arpeggio and Chord Progression

78 C D *p* *f* *mf*

March Slav

PETER ILYICH TCHAIKOVSKY
(1840–93)

79 Andante *ff* 1. 2.

Greensleeves

English Folk Song

80 Moderato *mp legato* *f* *rit.* *mp*

ADVANTAGE MUSICIANSHIP · Alma Mater

Traditional

81 Andante *p legato* Allegretto *rit.* *f a tempo* Adagio *rit.*

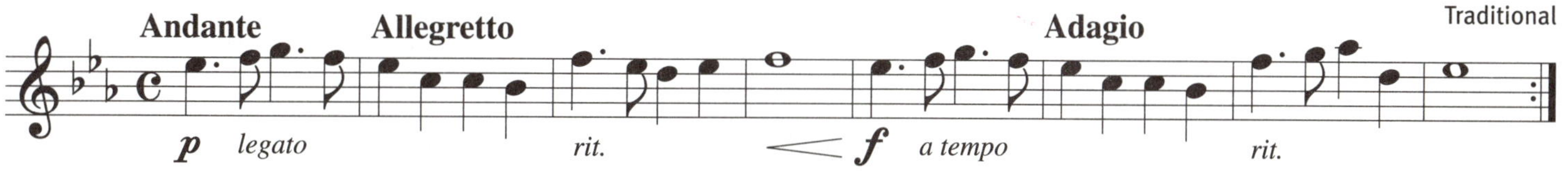

The Minstrel Boy
(Duet)

Irish Folk Song

82 1. Allegretto *f* 2. *f* 1. 2.

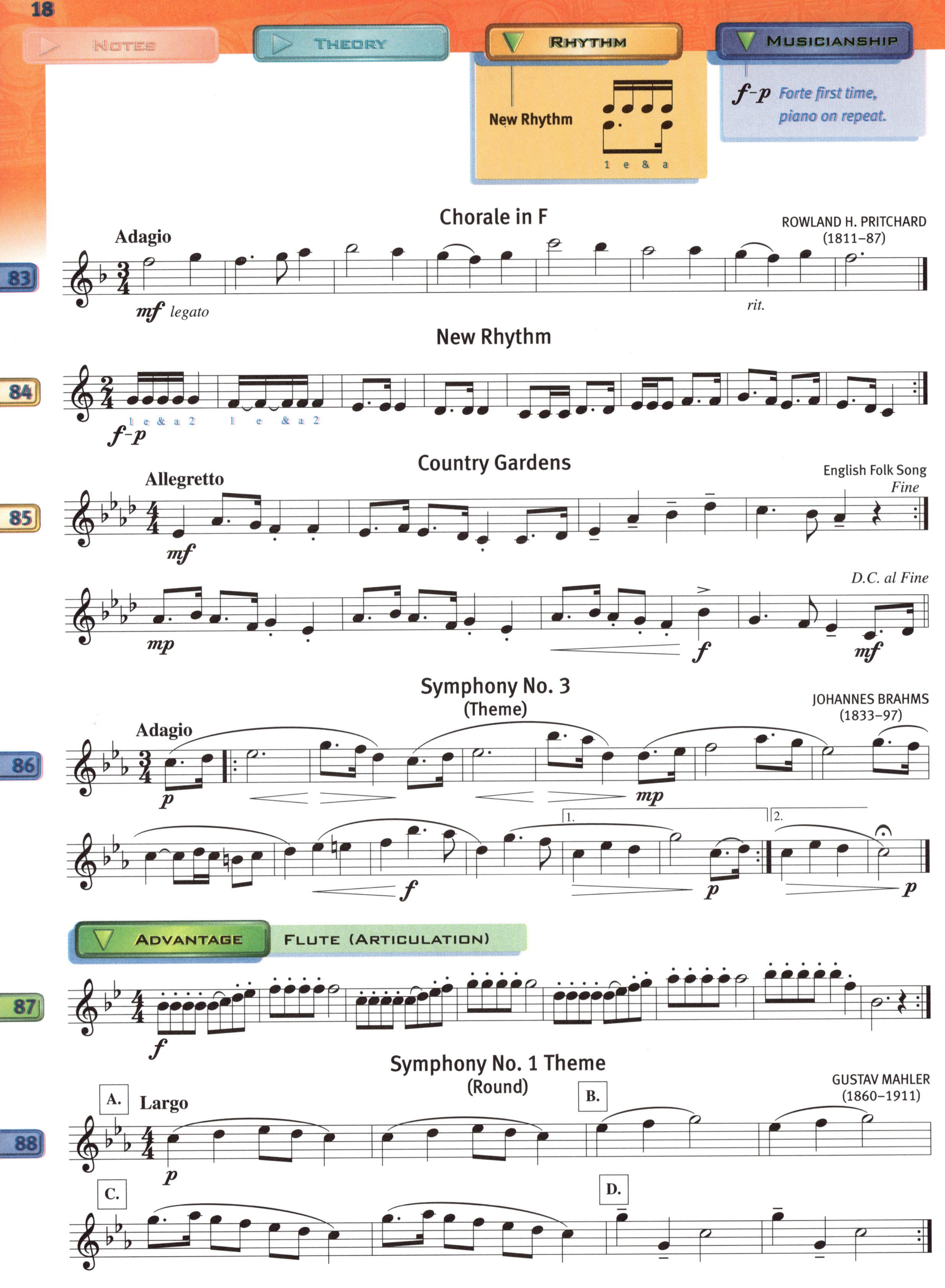

page 39 · Advantage Rhythm

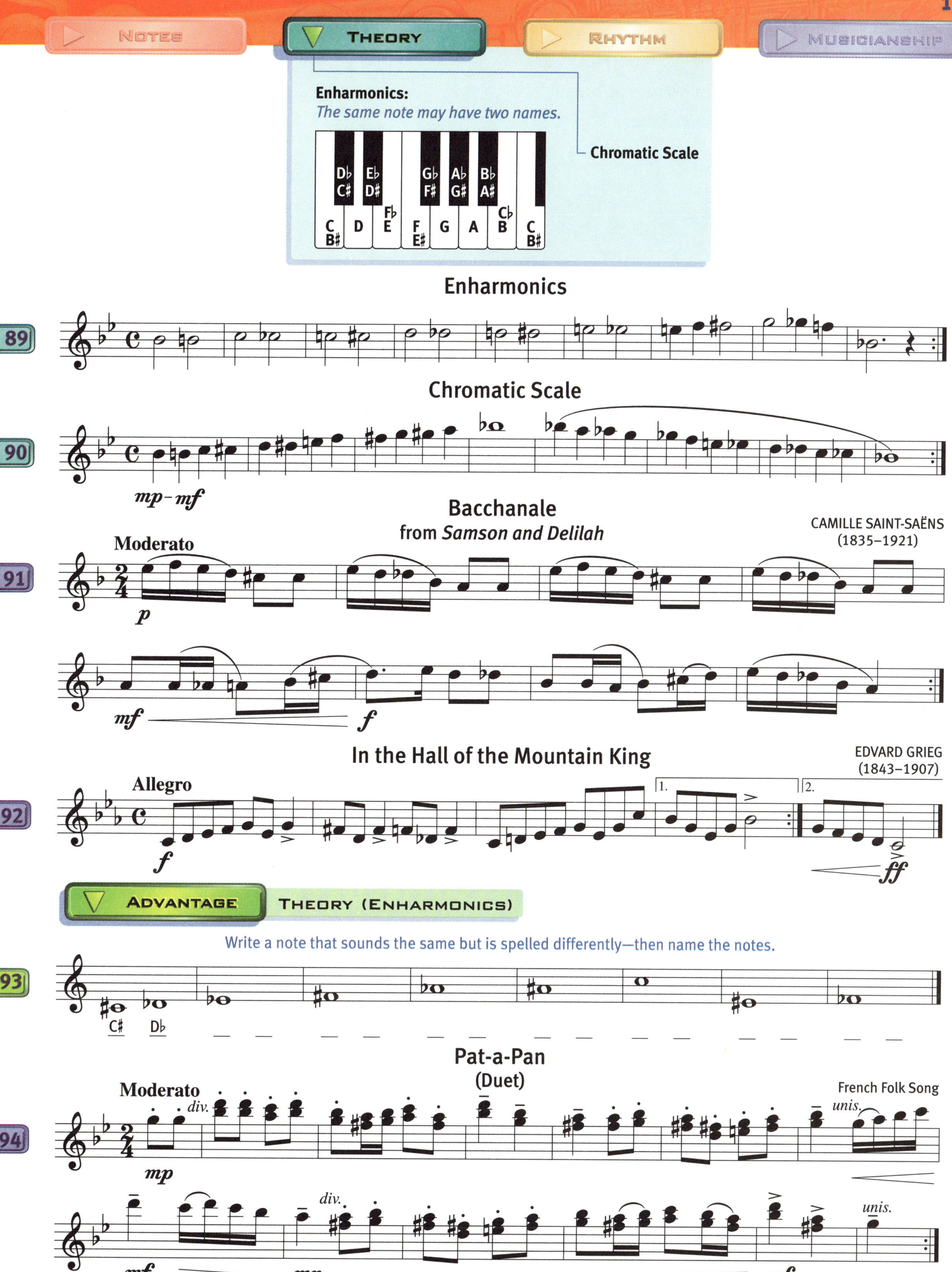
NOTES
THEORY
RHYTHM
MUSICIANSHIP
Enharmonics:
The same note may have two names.
D♭ C♯
E♭ D♯
G♭ F♯
A♭ G♯
B♭ A♯
C B♯
D
F♭ E
F E♯
G
A
C♭ B
C B♯
Chromatic Scale
Enharmonics
89
Chromatic Scale
90
mp – mf
Bacchanale
from Samson and Delilah
CAMILLE SAINT-SAËNS
(1835–1921)
Moderato
91
p
mf
f
In the Hall of the Mountain King
EDVARD GRIEG
(1843–1907)
Allegro
92
f
1.
2.
ff
ADVANTAGE
THEORY (ENHARMONICS)
Write a note that sounds the same but is spelled differently—then name the notes.
93
C♯
D♭
Pat-a-Pan
(Duet)
French Folk Song
Moderato
div.
unis.
94
mp
mf
mp
mf

Neighboring Tones

Chorale in A♭

PHILIP BLISS (1838–76)

95 

Technique Study

96 

Hatikvah

Israeli National Anthem

97 

March of the Toreadors

from *Carmen*

GEORGES BIZET (1838–75)

98 

ADVANTAGE COMPOSITION/IMPROVISATION

Neighboring tones are above or below a chord tone and immediately return to the chord tone.

Compose or improvise a melody using chord tones and neighboring tones.

99 

Minuet

(Duet)

LUDWIG van BEETHOVEN (1770–1827)

100 

page 41 · Advantage Flute

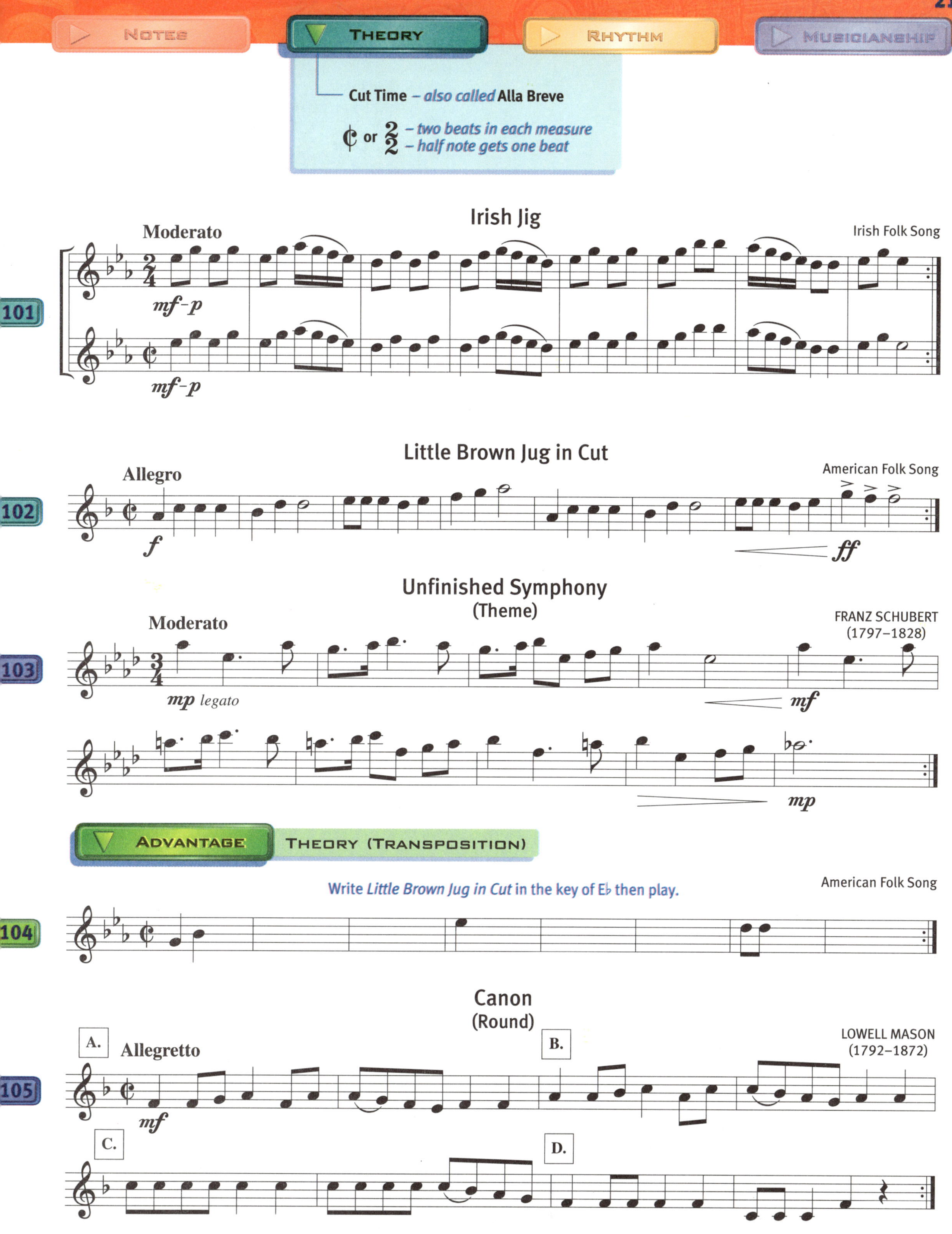

page 39 · Advantage Rhythm

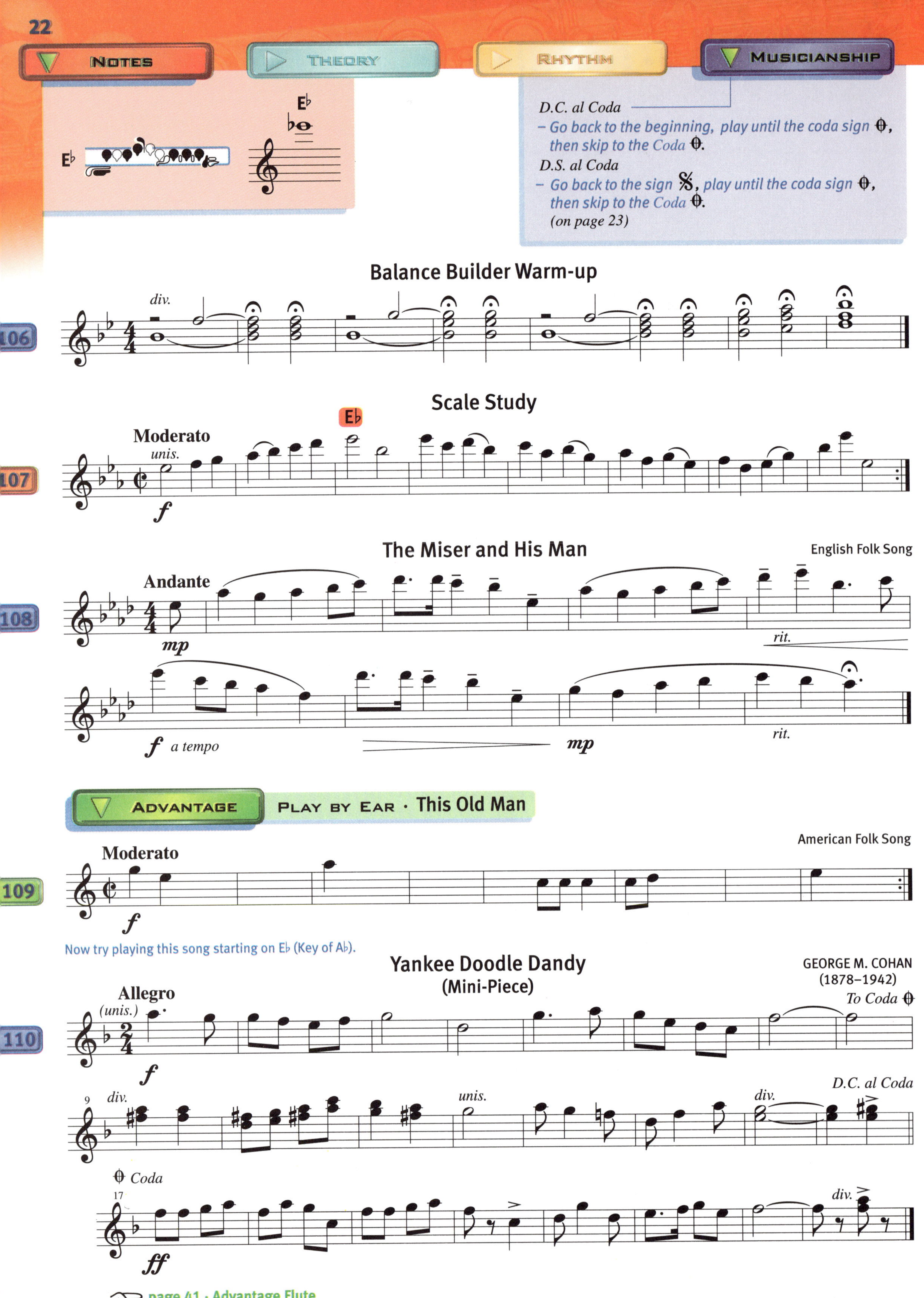

page 41 · Advantage Flute

PERFORMANCE

The American Patrol

FREDERICK W. MEACHAM
(ca.1850–95)
arranged by Sandy Feldstein & Larry Clark

Allegro 4 | 5 | second time only | *mf* | 6 | 7 | 8

div. | 9 | 10 | *unis.* | 11 | *div.* | 12 | *unis.* | 13 | 14

15 | 16 | 17 | 18 | *div.* | 19 | 1. Play | 20 | *mf* | 2. *unis.* | 21 | *f*

22 | 23 | 24 | 25 | 26 | 27 | 28 | 29 | *div.* | 30 | 31

32 | 33 | 34 | 35 | 36 | *To Coda* | 37

3 | 38 | second time only | *D.S. al Coda* | *unis.* | 41 | *mf* | Coda | 2 | 44 | *ff* | 45

Barbeque Strut

SANDY FELDSTEIN & LARRY CLARK
(b.1940) (b.1963)

Allegro 4 | 5 | second time only | 6 | 7 | 8 | 9

10 | *div.* | 1. Play | 11 | 12 | *f* | 2. | 13 | *unis.* | 14 | 15 | *div.*

16 | *unis.* | 17 | *div.* | 18 | *unis.* | 19 | *div.* | 20 | *unis.* | 21 | *div.* | 22 | *unis.* | *mf*

23 | 24 | 25 | 26 | 27 | 28 | *div.* | *To Coda*

29 | *unis.* | 30 | 31 | 32 | 33 | 34 | 35

36 | 37 | 38 | *D.S. al Coda* | Coda | *unis.* | 40 | 41 | 42 | *ff*

page 41 · Advantage Flute

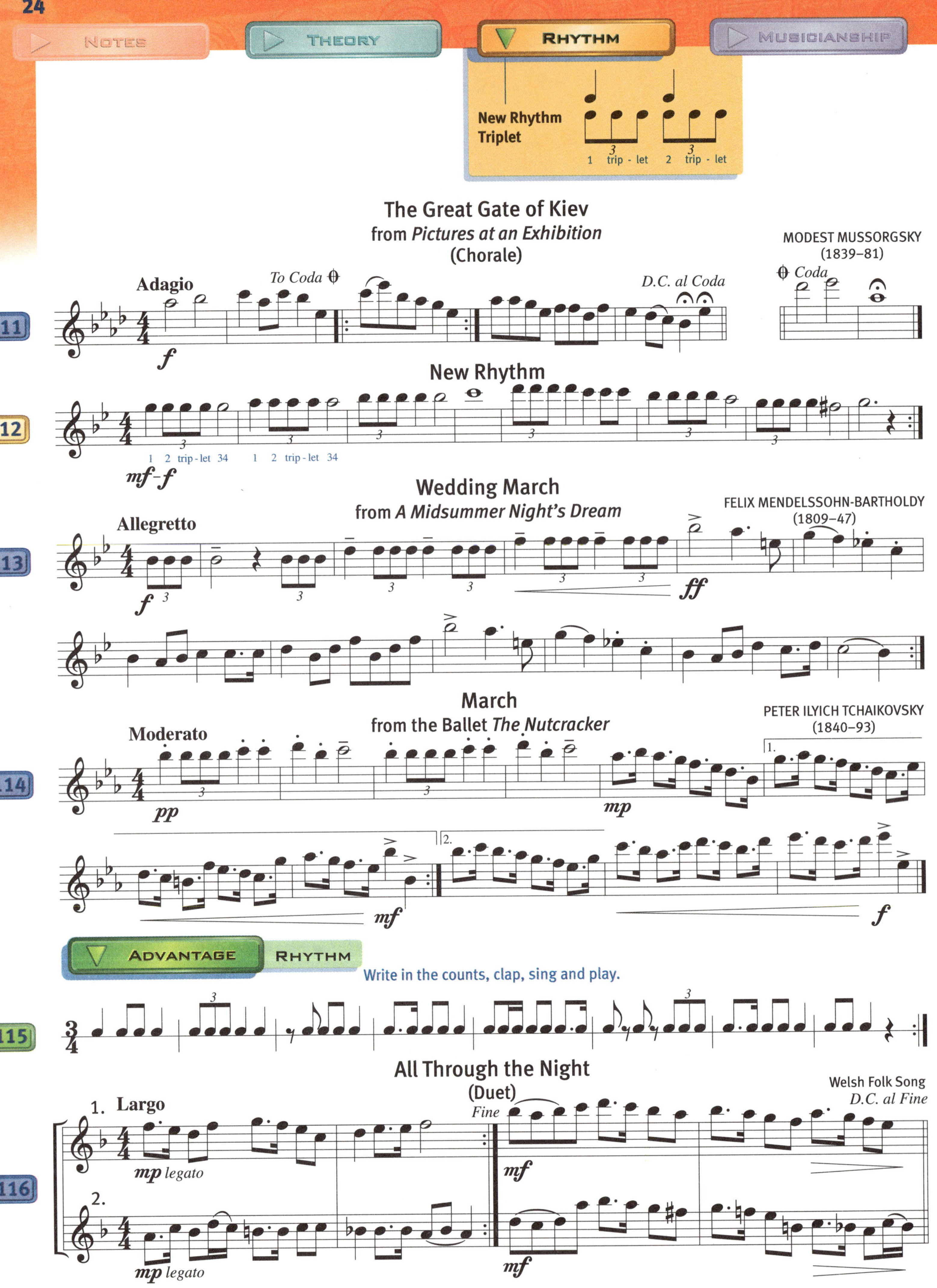

page 39 · Advantage Rhythm

page 41 · Advantage Flute

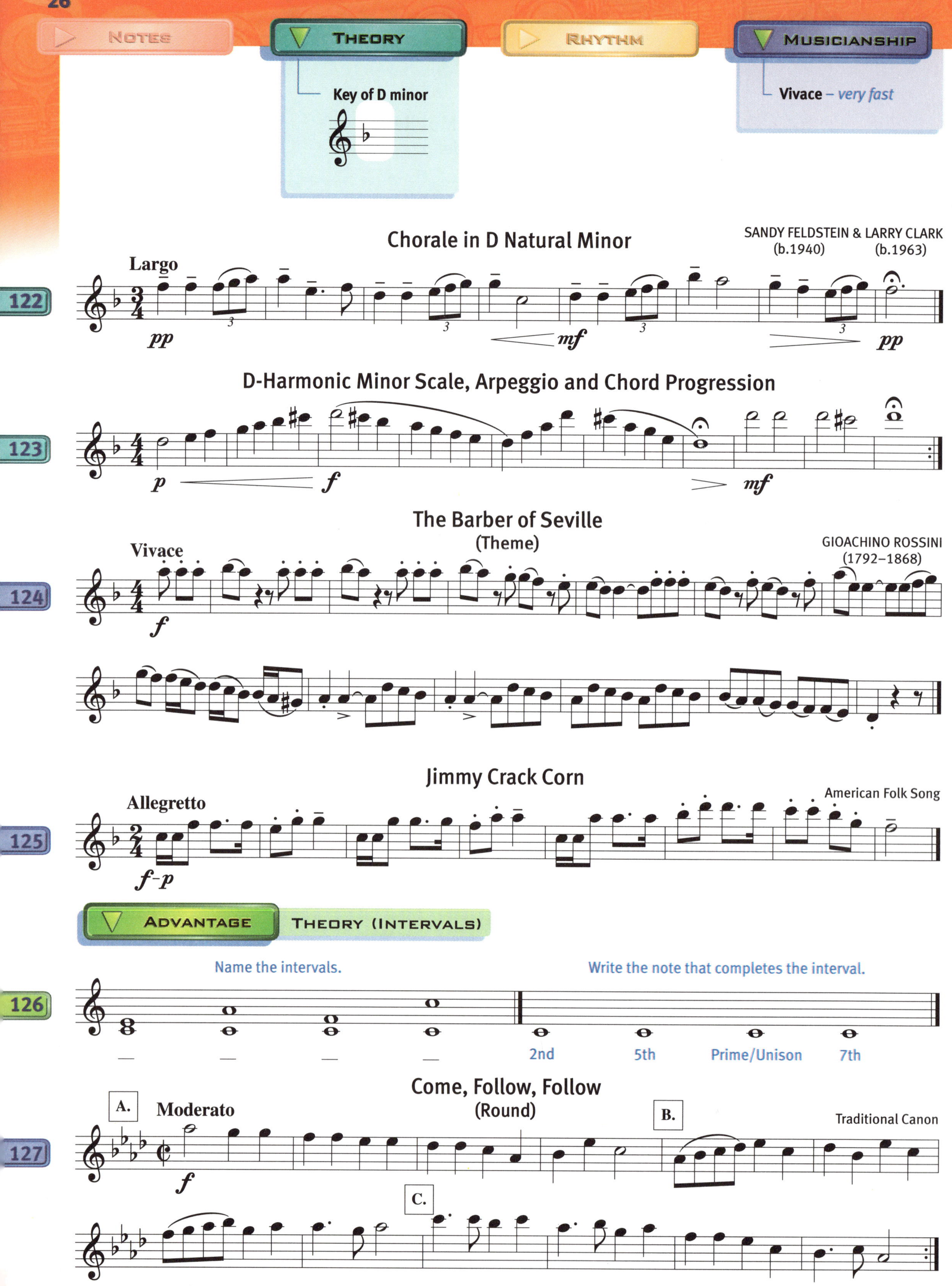
NOTES
THEORY
RHYTHM
MUSICIANSHIP
Key of D minor
Vivace – very fast
Chorale in D Natural Minor
SANDY FELDSTEIN & LARRY CLARK
(b.1940) (b.1963)
122
Largo
D-Harmonic Minor Scale, Arpeggio and Chord Progression
123
The Barber of Seville
(Theme)
GIOACHINO ROSSINI
(1792–1868)
124
Vivace
Jimmy Crack Corn
American Folk Song
125
Allegretto
ADVANTAGE
THEORY (INTERVALS)
126
Name the intervals.
Write the note that completes the interval.
2nd
5th
Prime/Unison
7th
Come, Follow, Follow
(Round)
Traditional Canon
127
A.
Moderato
B.
C.

THEORY

3 – three beats in each measure
8 – eighth note gets one beat

We Three Kings

Traditional Carol

28 Moderato

mf

f

All the Pretty Little Horses

American Folk Song

29 Adagio

p

Fine

D.C. al Fine

Take Me Out to the Ballgame

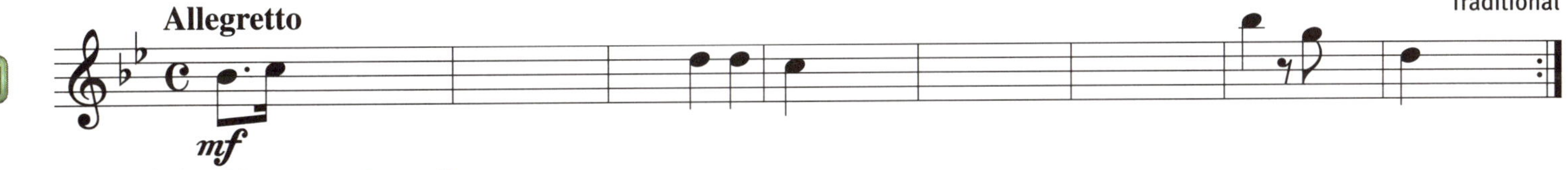

Now try playing this song starting on C.

Chopsticks

(Duet)

Traditional

32 1. Allegretto

p

mf

f

2.

p

mf

f

page 39 · Advantage Rhythm

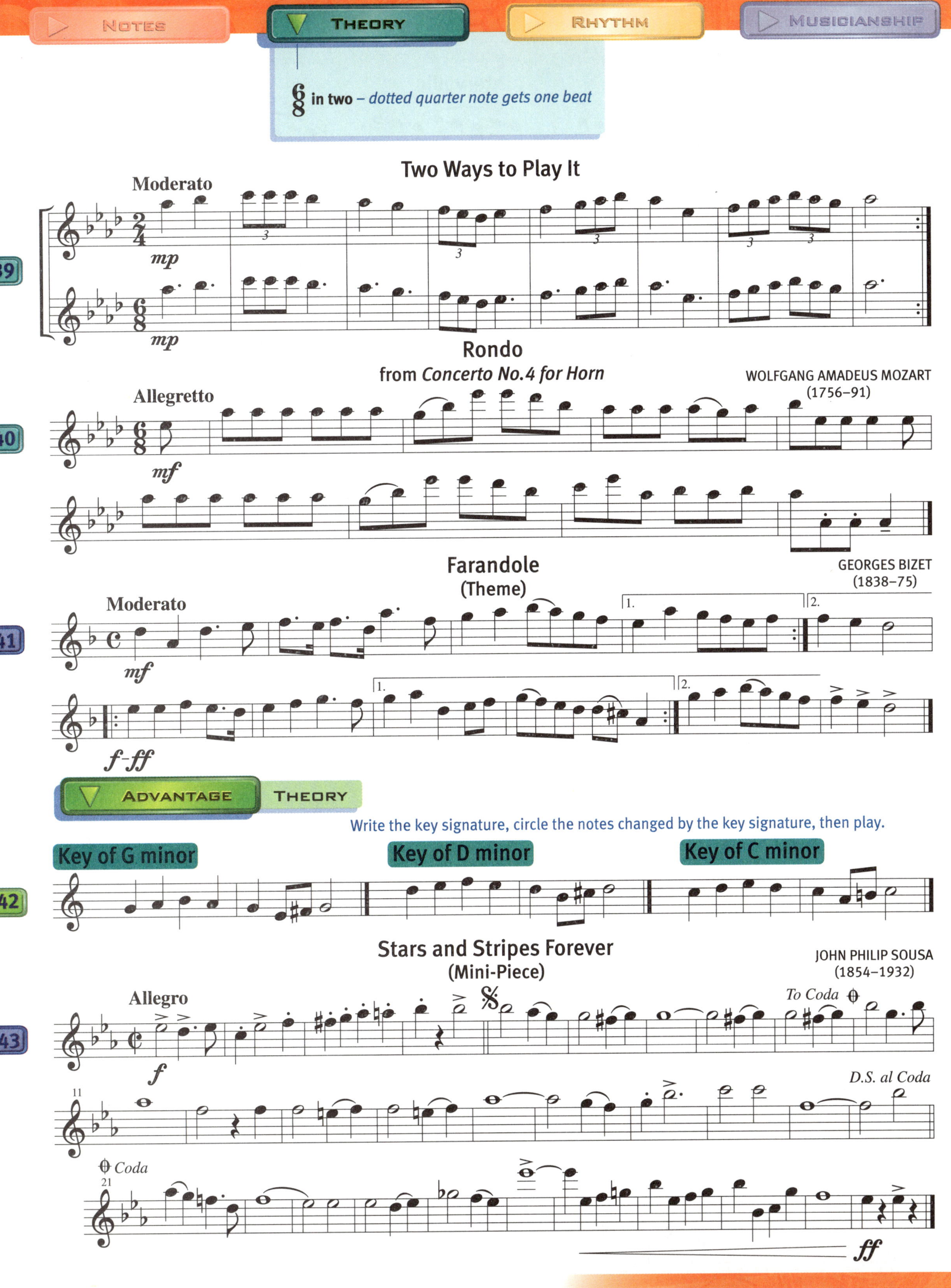
NOTES
THEORY
RHYTHM
MUSICIANSHIP
6/8 in two – dotted quarter note gets one beat
Two Ways to Play It
Moderato
39
mp
mp
Rondo
from Concerto No.4 for Horn
WOLFGANG AMADEUS MOZART
(1756–91)
Allegretto
40
mf
Farandole
(Theme)
GEORGES BIZET
(1838–75)
Moderato
41
mf
f-ff
ADVANTAGE
THEORY
Write the key signature, circle the notes changed by the key signature, then play.
Key of G minor
Key of D minor
Key of C minor
42
Stars and Stripes Forever
(Mini-Piece)
JOHN PHILIP SOUSA
(1854–1932)
Allegro
43
f
To Coda
D.S. al Coda
Coda
ff

Intervallic
SANDY FELDSTEIN & LARRY CLARK
(b.1940) (b.1963)
Andante
To Coda
Allegro
legato
D.C. al Coda
Coda
rit.
Ye Banks and Braes
Scottish Folk Song
arranged by Sandy Feldstein & Larry Clark
Adagio
rit.
Allegro
second time only
Both times
div.

NOTES
THEORY
RHYTHM
MUSICIANSHIP
E
F
New Note Warm-up
44
unis.
pp p mp mf f mf ff
Scale Study
45
Largo
f
Semper Fidelis
JOHN PHILIP SOUSA
(1854–1932)
46
Allegro
f
The Entertainer
SCOTT JOPLIN
(1868–1917)
47
Allegretto
Solo/Soli
mf
Tutti
To Coda
Solo/Soli
Tutti
D.C. al Coda
Coda
f
ADVANTAGE
RHYTHM
Add in the bar lines, write in the counts, clap, sing and play.
48
White Coral Bells
(Round)
English Folk Song
49
A.
Moderato
B.
mf

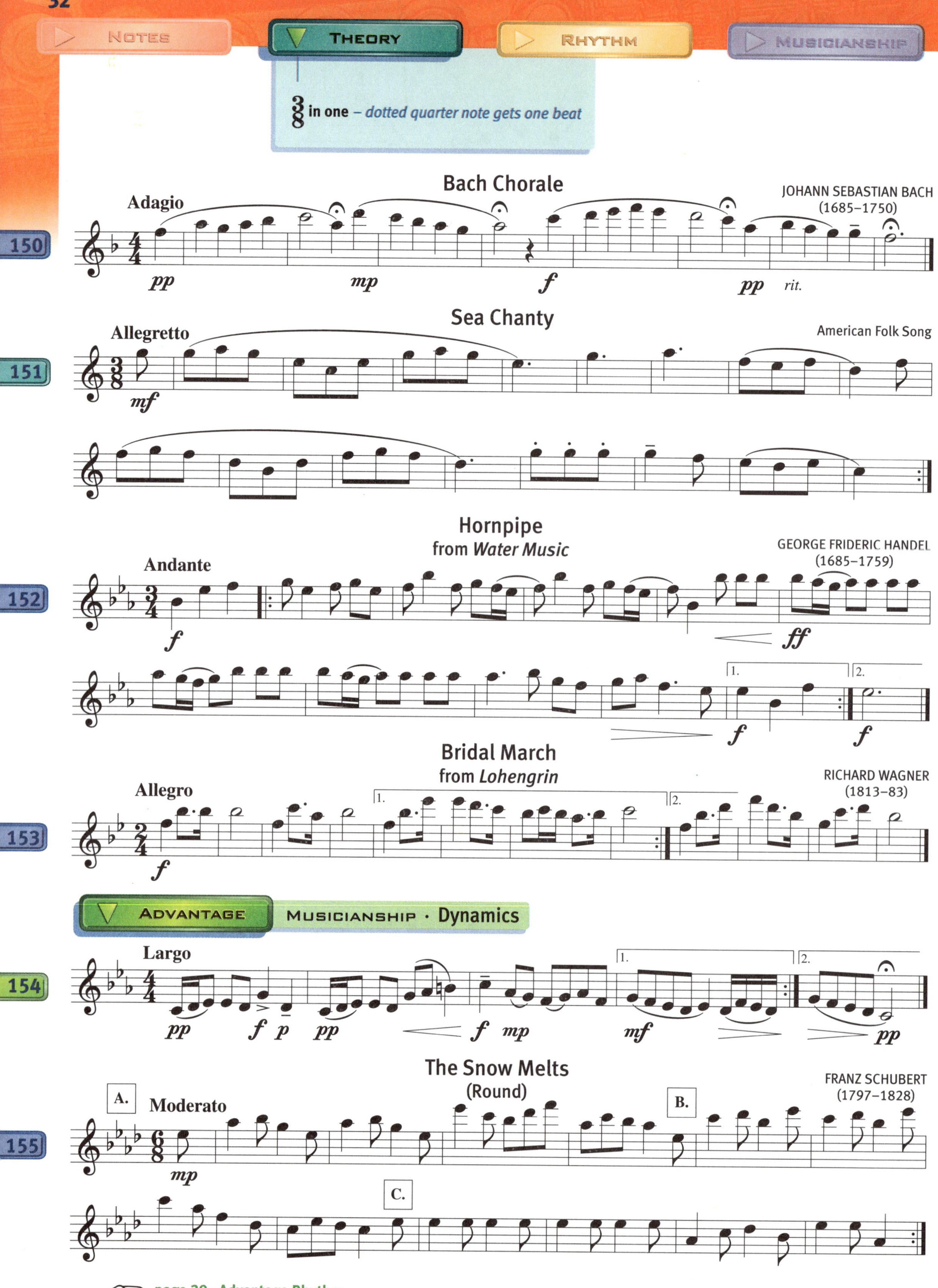

page 39 · Advantage Rhythm

Woltok
Moderato
Polish Folk Song
56
f-p
Hungarian Dance No. 5
Vivace
JOHANNES BRAHMS
(1833–97)
57
ff
p
ff
Sailor's Song
Allegretto
English Folk Song
58
mf
1.
2.
f
mf
ADVANTAGE
FLUTE (CHROMATIC)
59
f
Spinning Song
(Duet)
Allegro
ALBERT ELLMENREICH
(1816–1905)
60
div.
unis.
div.
Fine
f a tempo on D.C.
1.
2.
D.C. al Fine
unis.
mp
mf
rit.

Andante Cantabile

FRANZ JOSEPH HAYDN
(1732–1809)

f
p
pp
rit.

Andante Cantabile

FRANZ JOSEPH HAYDN
(1732–1809)

PERFORMANCE

Equinox

SANDY FELDSTEIN & LARRY CLARK
(b.1940) (b.1963)

Allegro

f

9

mp

17

25

32

mf f mf f ff mf f

div. unis.

41 Faster

mf ff f unis.

1.

mp mf

2.

div.

58 Adagio

unis.

ff

64 Vivace

rit. f

mf f ff

After page 3

Andante

R1 — 2/4 — *p* — 1. *f* — 2. *f*

After page 4

Allegro

R2 — 4/4 — *mf* — *mp* — *mf* — *mp* — *f*

After page 5

Moderato

R3 — 3/4 — *f* — 𝄋 — *Fine* — *p* — *D.S. al Fine*

After page 6

Largo

R4 — C — *mp* — *f* — *Fine* — *D.C. al Fine*

After page 8

Allegro

R5 — 2/4 — *f* — *p* — *mp* — 1. *mf* — 2. *mf* — *f*

After page 10

Moderato

R6 — 3/4 — *mf* — *rit.* — *p a tempo* — *f*

After page 11

Andante

R7 — 2/4 — *ff* — *p* — *ff*

After page 13

Adagio

R8 — 4/4 — *pp* — *ff* — 1. — 2.

After page 15

Allegretto

R9 — 2/4 — *mf* — *f* — *ff*

ADVANTAGE

RHYTHM

After page 18

Allegro

10
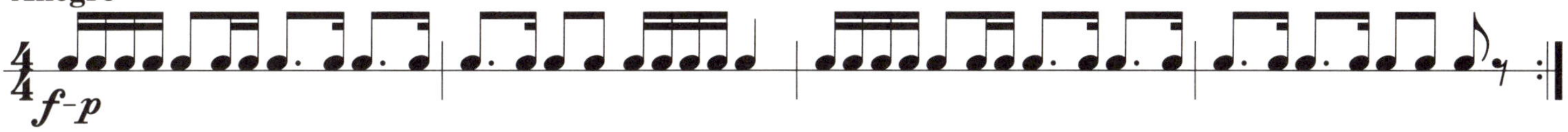
f-p

After page 19

Andante

12
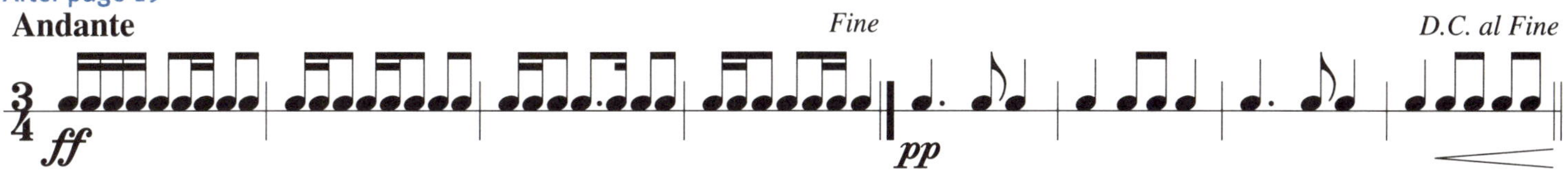
Fine
D.C. al Fine
ff
pp

After page 21

Allegretto

13
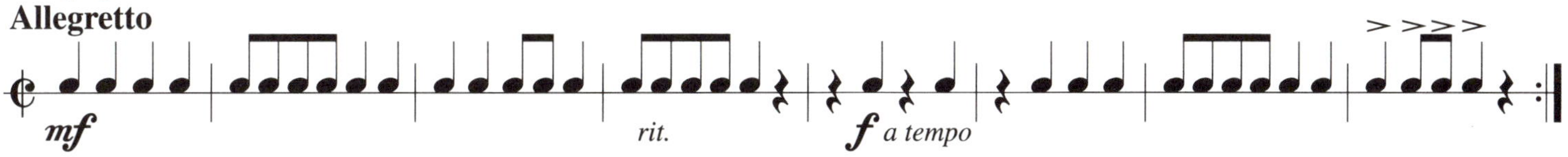
mf
rit.
f a tempo

After page 24

Moderato

14
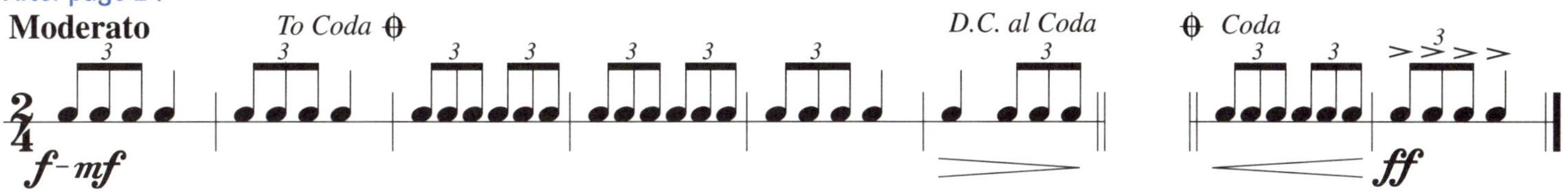
To Coda
D.C. al Coda
Coda
f-mf
ff

After page 27

Andante

15
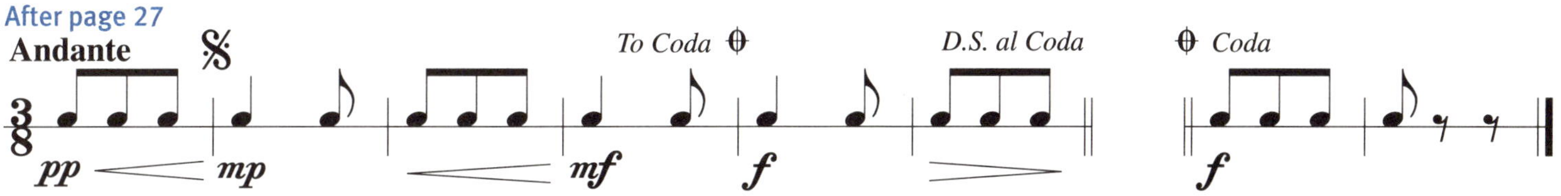
To Coda
D.S. al Coda
Coda
pp
mp
mf
f
f

After page 28

Largo

16
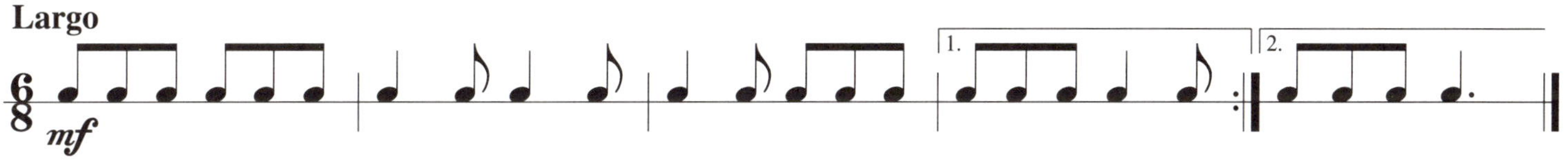
1.
2.
mf

After page 29

Vivace

17
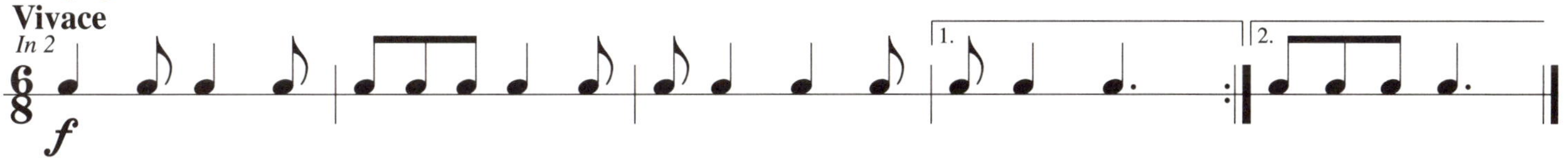
In 2
1.
2.
f

After page 32

Vivace

18
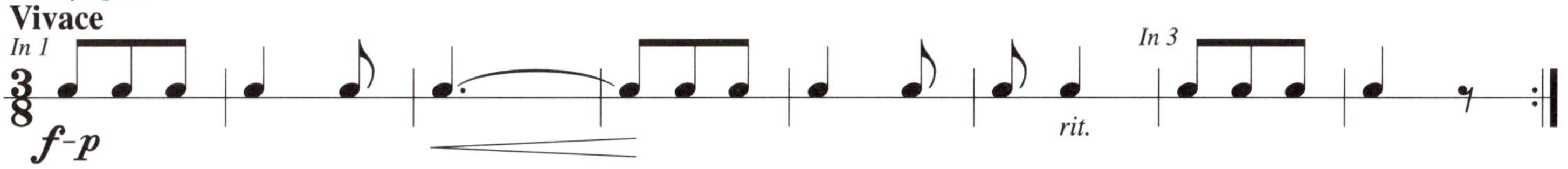
In 1
In 3
f-p
rit.

After page 33

Adagio

19
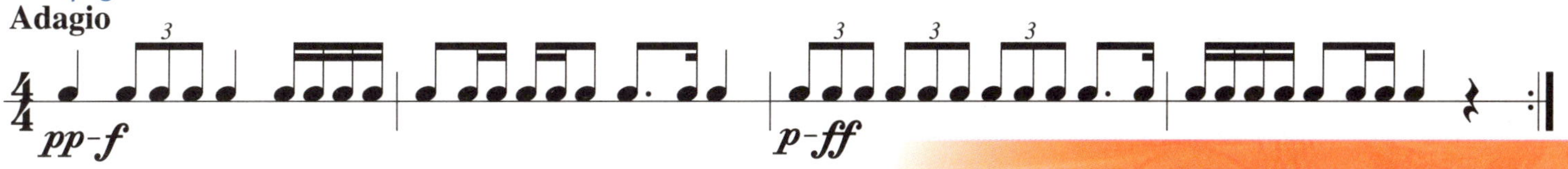
pp-f
p-ff

After page 2

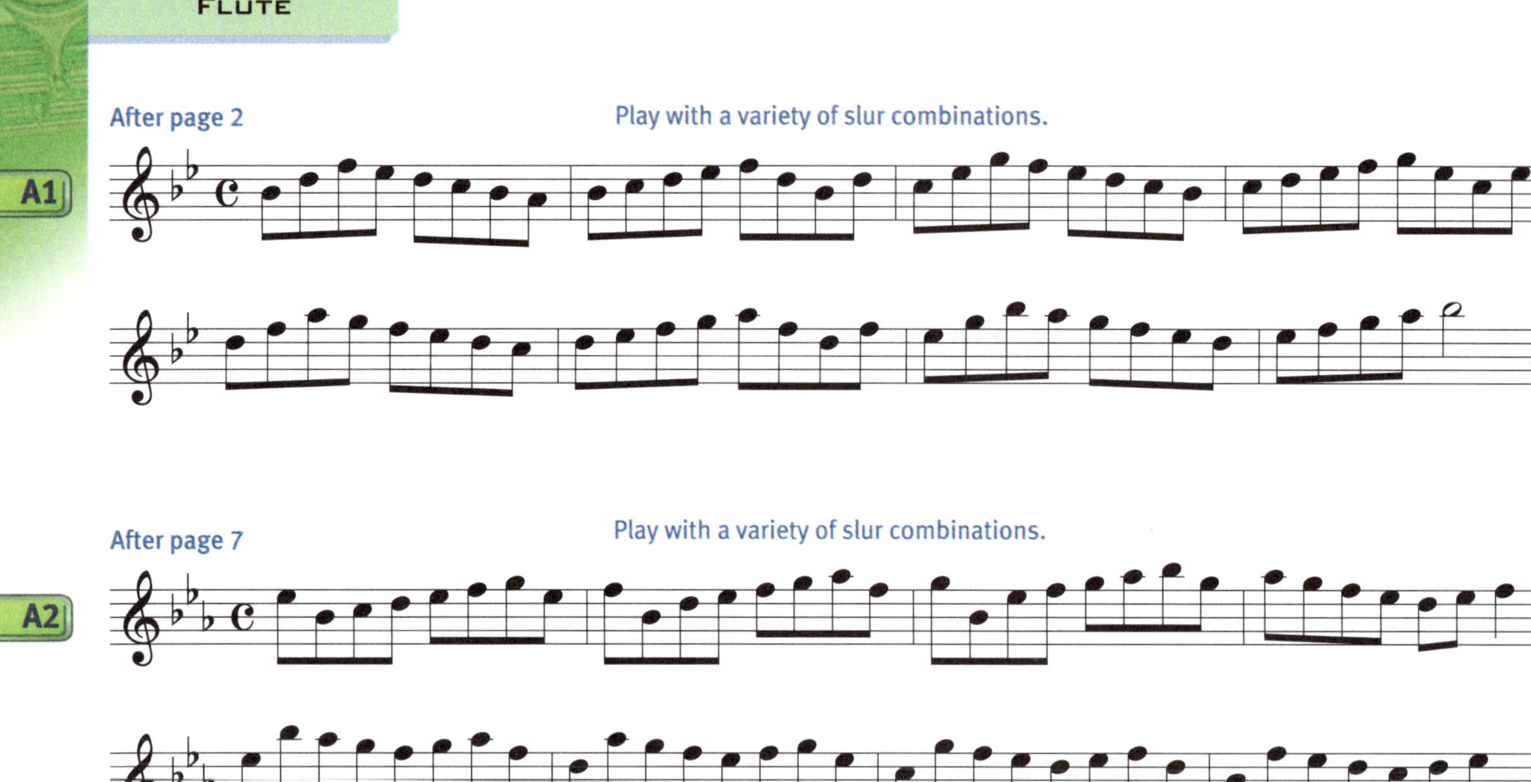

After page 12

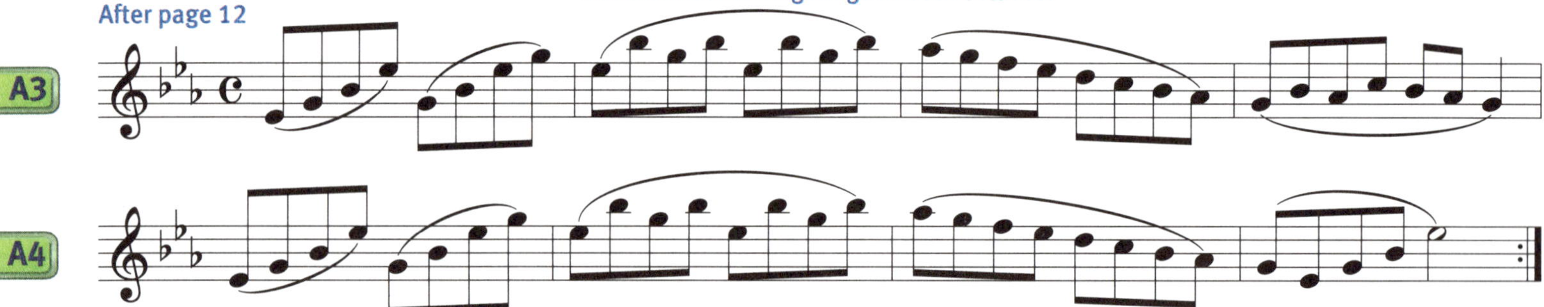

After page 15

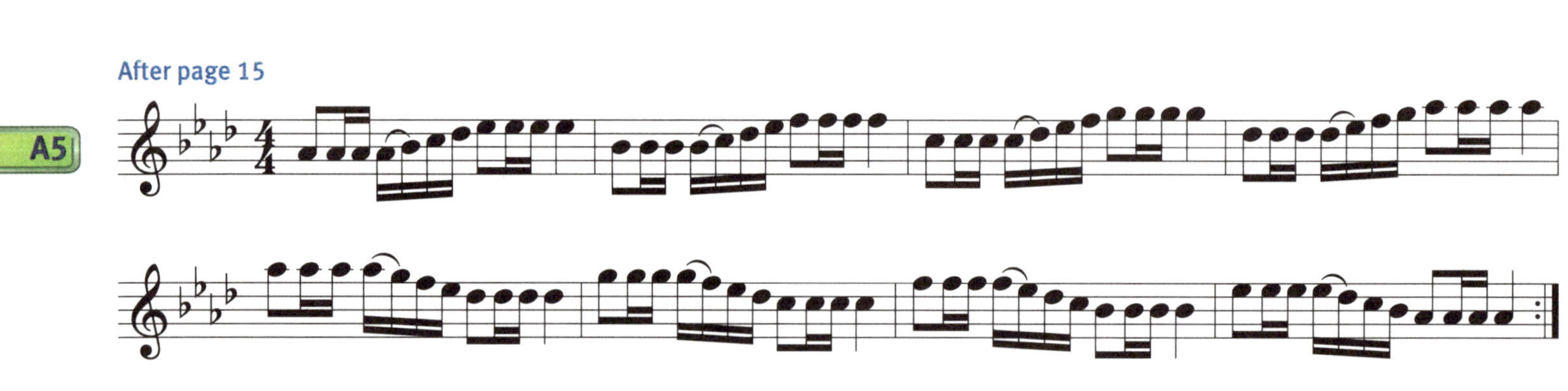

After page 19

Finger lower note throughout, then continue down to low C.
D. SCHMIDT
from *My First Wagner*
After page 22
A7
After page 23
Play with a variety of slur combinations.
A8
After page 25
G. PARÈS
A9
After page 27
Continue up on each note of the F-Major scale.
10
3 3 3 3
After page 29
Try playing this pattern in other keys.
E. WAGNER
11
After page 33
12

ADVANTAGE
THEORY (SCALES)
Circle of fourths / fifths
C
G
F
5ths
4ths
D
B♭
A
E♭
E
(F♭)
A♭
B
(C♭)
G♭
(F♯)
D♭
(C♯)
Practice all scales in cut-time as well.
C-Major Scale
Arpeggio
T1
Thirds
F-Major Scale
Arpeggio
T2
Thirds
B♭-Major Scale
Arpeggio
T3
Thirds
E♭-Major Scale
Arpeggio
T4
Thirds
A♭-Major Scale
Arpeggio
T5

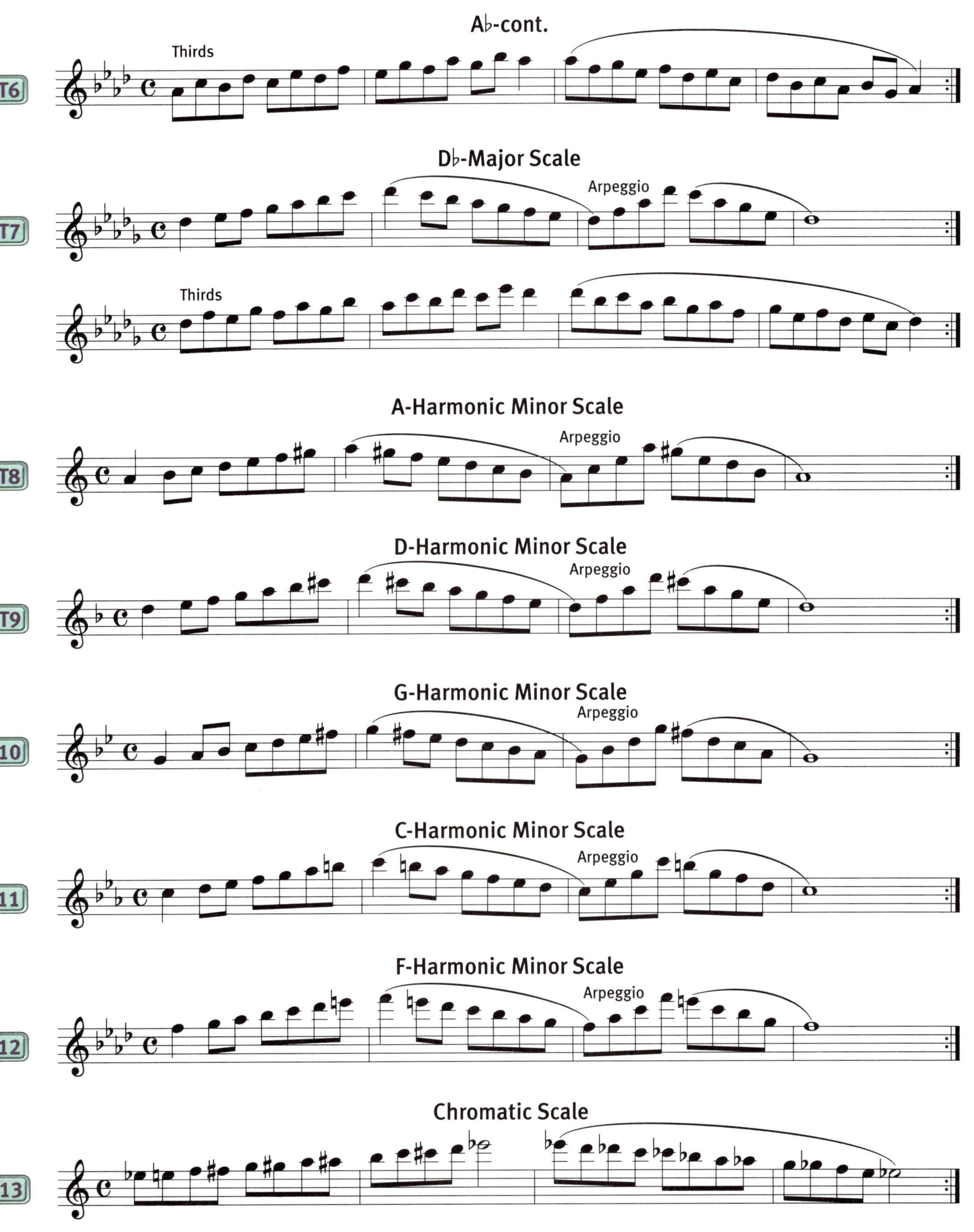
A♭-cont.
Thirds
T6
D♭-Major Scale
Arpeggio
T7
Thirds
A-Harmonic Minor Scale
Arpeggio
T8
D-Harmonic Minor Scale
Arpeggio
T9
G-Harmonic Minor Scale
Arpeggio
T10
C-Harmonic Minor Scale
Arpeggio
T11
F-Harmonic Minor Scale
Arpeggio
T12
Chromatic Scale
T13

Theory Review

Name the upper neighbors (U), the lower neighbors (L), and passing tones (P).

T13 

Scale Review

Write the A♭-major scale, indicate the whole and half steps, write the note names, then fill in the missing notes of the A♭ chord.

T14 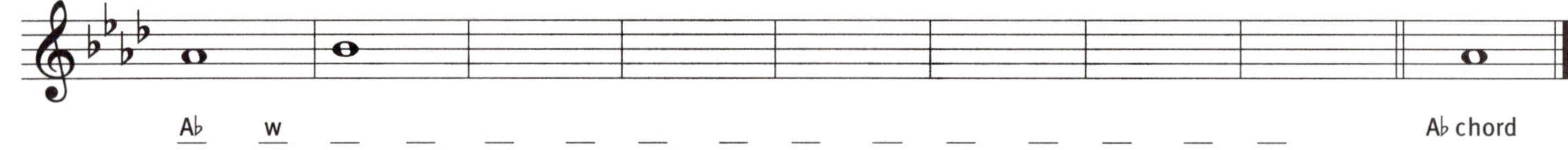

Write the key signature for a D-minor scale, then write the scale.

T15 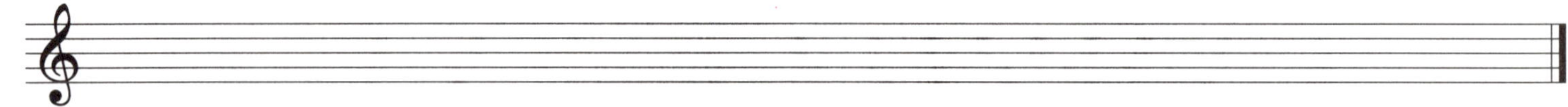

Rhythm Review

Write the counts, clap, sing and play.

In 3

T16 

In 2

T17 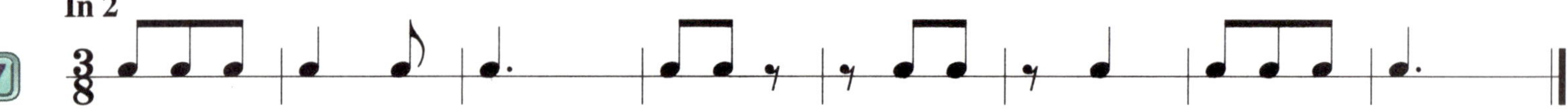

In 6

T18 

In 2

T19 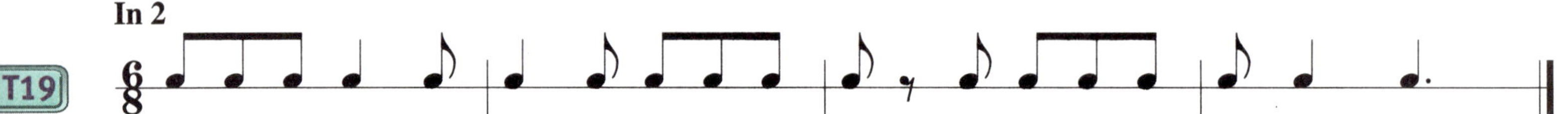

T20 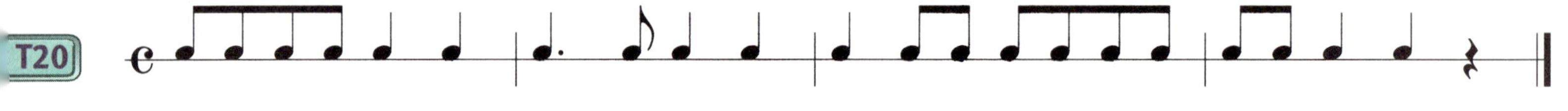

T21 

ADVANTAGE

MUSICAL TERMS

1st and 2nd endings	Play the 1st ending first time through, then on the repeat, skip to the 2nd ending.
a tempo	Return to the previous tempo.
Accent	Play the note stronger, with more emphasis.
Adagio	A slow tempo between Andante and Largo.
Allegretto	Moderately fast tempo.
Allegro	Fast tempo.
Andante	Moderately slow tempo.
Bass clef	Also called F clef. The fourth line of the staff is the note F.
Canon	Another name for a round.
Chorale	A hymn tune usually lyrical.
Chord	Three or more notes played at the same time.
Chord Progression	The movement of one chord to another.
Chromatic scale	A scale consisting of only half steps.
Common time C	Same as 4/4 time signature.
Crescendo	Gradually increase volume.
Cut time (Alla Breve)	¢ or 2/2 - Two beats per measure, the half note gets one beat.
D.C. al Coda	Go back to the beginning, play until the coda sign then skip to the *Coda*.
D.S. al Coda	Go back to the sign 𝄋,play until the coda sign , then skip to the *Coda*.
D.C. (Da Capo) al Fine	*D.C. al fine* Go back to the beginning and play until Fine.
D.S. (Dal Segno) al Fine	*D.S. al fine* Go back to the 𝄋 sign and play until Fine.
Decrescendo	Gradually decrease volume.
Divisi *div.*	Divided section with some players playing the top notes while others play the bottom.
Dot	Increases the value of the original note by one half.
Enharmonics	Notes that have different names but sound the same (i.e. C♯ = D♭)
Fermata 𝄐	Hold the note longer than its usual value.
Fine	The end.
Flat ♭	Lowers a note one half step.
Form	The structure of a composition.
Forte *f*	Loud.
Fortissimo *ff*	Very loud.
Interval	Distance between two notes.
Introduction	A preparation section to a composition.
Key signature	Shows the notes that are flat or sharp within a piece.
Largo	Very slow.
Ledger lines	Used to extend the staff.
Legato	Play the notes smoothly with a soft tongue.
Major Scale	A scale pattern consisting of whole steps (w) and half steps (h). Pattern - w-w-h-w-w-w-h
Measure	The distance between two bar lines.
Mezzo Forte *mf*	Medium loud.
Mezzo Piano *mp*	Medium soft.
Minor Scale	A scale starting on the sixth scale degree of a major scale.
Moderato	Moderate tempo.
Multiple measure rest	Indicates more than one measure of rest.
Natural ♮	Cancels a flat or sharp, stays in effect for the entire measure.
Phrase, Phrasing	A complete musical statement.
Pianissimo *pp*	Very soft.
Piano *p*	Soft.
Pick-up note(s)	Note(s) preceding the first full measure, the missing beats may appear in the last measure.
Play by Ear	Play melodies without looking at written notation.
Repeat Sign	Play the music again from the beginning.
Repeat within a piece	Repeat only the music between the signs.
Ritardando *rit.*	Gradually slow down.
Round	Playing the same music starting at different times.
Scale	The arrangement of notes within a tonal setting.
Sharp ♯	Raises a note one half step, stays in effect for the entire measure.
Syncopation	Accents on weak beats.
Slur	A curved line placed above or below a group of notes to indicate that they are played smooth and connected. Tongue only the first note of a slur.
Soli	A solo for more than one instrument.
Solo	One person playing.
Staccato	Play the note lightly and separated.
Tenuto	Play full value.
Theme & Variations	A musical form where the rhythm or notes of a theme are changed to create variety.
Theory	The study of the components of musical composition.
Tie	Joins two notes of the same pitch, played as if they were one.
Time signature	Indicates how many beats are in each measure and what kind of note receives one beat.
Treble Clef	Also called G clef. The second line of the staff is the note G.
Tutti	Everyone plays.
Transposition	Changing a song to a different key.
Unison *unis.*	All players in the section play the same note.
Vivace	Very fast tempo.

Advantage

Fingerings

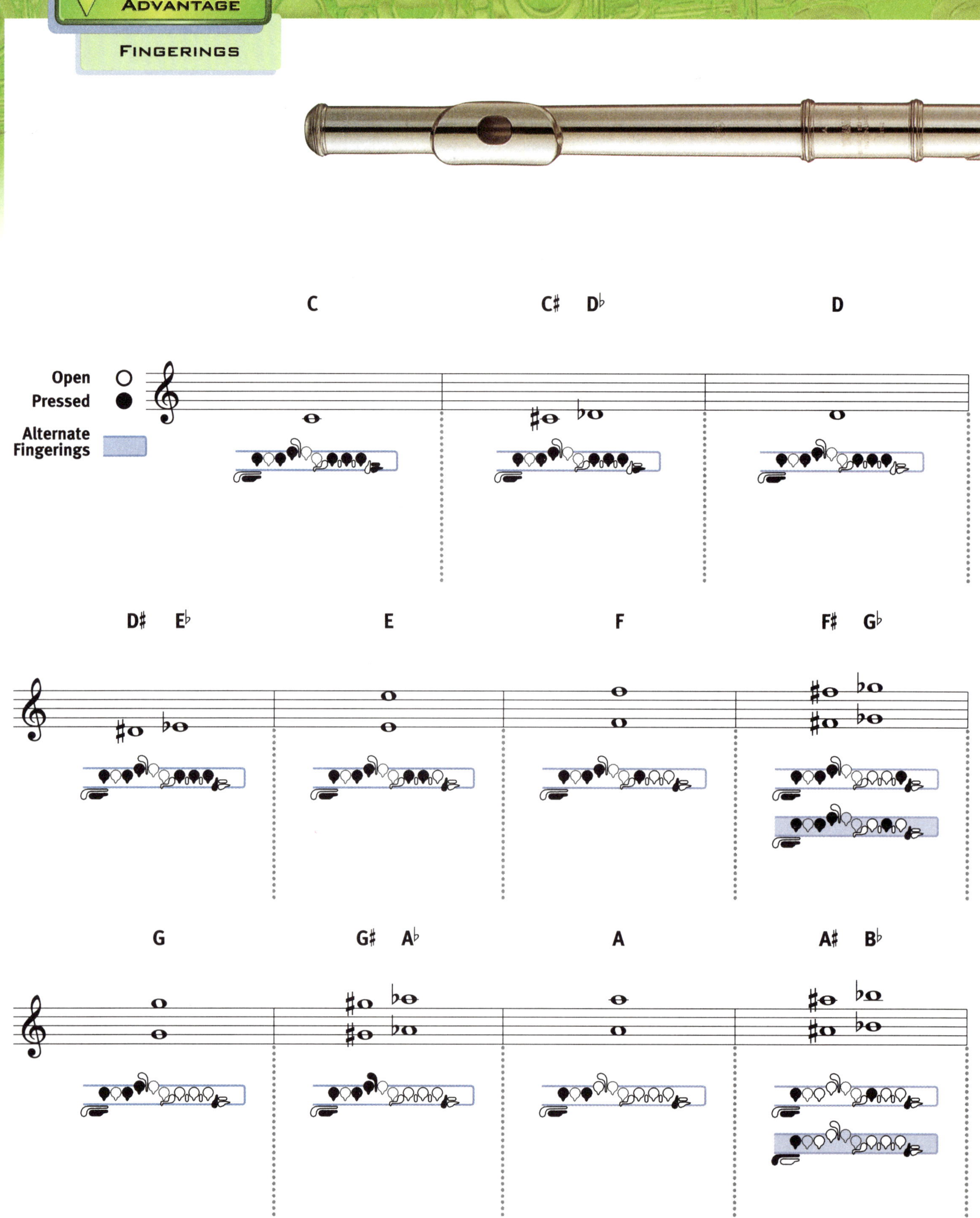

The following products are recommended for complete care of your instrument:

Cleaning Gauze · Cork Grease · Flute Cleaning Rod · Key Oil · Linen Swab · Pad Cleaning Paper · Polishing Cloth · Tone Hole Cleaner

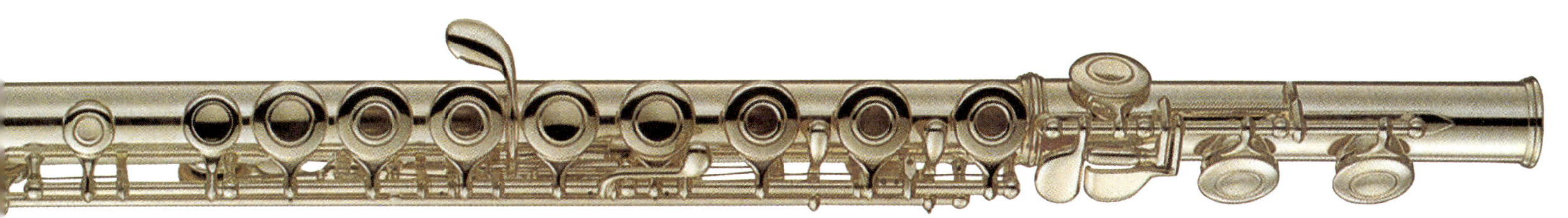

B

C

C♯ D♭

D

D♯ E♭

D

D♯ E♭

E

F

F♯ G♭

G

Date	Teacher · Assignments/Goals	Student · Notes/Questions	Mon.	Tues.	Wed.	Thurs.	Fri.	Sat.	Sun.	Approval